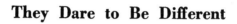

They Dare to Be Different

Books by ELMER G. LETERMAN

COMMISSIONS DON'T FALL FROM HEAVEN
HOW SHOWMANSHIP SELLS
NEW ART OF SELLING
PERSONAL POWER THROUGH CREATIVE SELLING
THE SALE BEGINS WHEN THE CUSTOMER SAYS NO

They Dare to Be Different

by

ELMER G. LETERMAN

and

THOMAS W. CARLIN

MEREDITH PRESS / New York

TO

NORMAN N. GORTZ

First edition

Library of Congress Catalog Card Number: 68-9518

MANUFACTURED IN THE UNITED STATES OF AMERICA FOR MEREDITH PRESS

VAN REES PRESS • NEW YORK

Contents

Elmer Leterman

Before Christopher Columbus presented himself to the Queen of Spain with his revolutionary idea of sailing west to reach Asia, he made a vain appeal for support to the Senate of his native State of Genoa. Stephen Jenks, former executive vice-president of United States Steel Corporation, explains what happened in these words:

The Senate in Genoa, knowing little of such things, made a truly modern response to Columbus' proposal—they appointed a committee to study the idea. The committee, of course, wrote a report which recently came to light in a monastery library in southeastern Spain. What a report it was! It ran on for 964 pages.

The committee then sent Columbus a letter summarizing its conclusions. After suggesting several further studies and discouraging the westward voyage, the committee's letter ended as follows: "We feel that you will be quite pleased with the output of this progressive, forward-looking committee of profound scholars. Incidentally, there was one rather rash and impetuous young engineer, lately of Florence, who was sent in place of the ailing Dr. Taglotti of the University of Milan. Though he came highly recommended, he showed his immaturity and poor judgment by advocating that the voyage itself be initiated immediately.

Investigation proved him to be quite eccentric (he

talks of flying machines and fancies himself an artist),
and he was therefore dismissed from the committee. He
is the son of a Florentine notary and, in case you desire
to contact him, his name is Leonardo da Vinci."

This book tells the stories of several modern-day Leonardo
da Vincis. Its thesis is simple: In a society overrun by people
trying to be carbon copies of one another, anyone with the
nerve and verve to be different can lead an exciting life filled
with a sense of personal satisfaction. The stories of these men
and women stand as testaments not only to their achievements
but also to the singular courage they exhibit in being willing
to stand out from the crowd.

I am reminded of a paragraph from a recent letter that I
received from Joseph S. Sparks, a fellow member of the New-
comen Society:

I'll never forget my first glimpse of you at last night's
dinner. The ballroom was filled with elite business
leaders of the country, each dressed in midnight blue
tuxedos topped with starched white shirts. Each, that is,
except one! Elmer Leterman, standing out from the
others like a diamond from its setting, was bedecked
in a gray silk formalwear with black satin trim. I can't
tell you how much I admire you for your courage to be
different.

That particular tuxedo accomplished its purpose. Because
it was different, it generated a great deal of good-natured
ribbing. It served as a springboard to my meeting several
important people who otherwise might not have noticed or
remembered me.

Clothes are one of my trademarks. I experiment constantly
with new styles. However, I do not believe in overstepping
the boundaries of good taste. Whenever I dream up a new

design, I consult with my sister-in-law, Jo Copeland, the famous designer. She has the infallible ability of keeping me on track.

Unusual clothes, of course, are an excellent vehicle for gaining fairly widespread publicity. In point of fact, the tuxedo was written up together with a full-page color photo in *Gentleman's Quarterly*. It was also mentioned by two New York columnists, and in an article in *Salesman's Magazine*. I made four thousand reprints of each of these items, half for distribution to people on my personal mailing list, half to hand out to people I meet during the course of my daily rounds.

I learned the conversational and publicity value of wearing unusual clothes when I was an eighteen-year-old apprentice salesman in the garment district of Manhattan. For months, I had been trying my darnedest to look, act, and sound like the older salesmen I saw while making my rounds. I felt that, if I could somehow become a mirror-image of those established salesmen, I would start to get a share of business commensurate with my efforts. I was particularly discouraged because I knew that the materials I sold were of the highest quality. I knew that if somehow I could gain a really favorable hearing I would be on my way to success.

Each day my spirits ebbed a little more as I limped along with lackluster sales results. I had the feeling that buyers were looking right through me and weren't even listening to what I said. After each call, I held mental postmortems, trying to figure some way to gain control of the presentations I was making. I realized almost instinctively that I had to do something to make these people react to me as a person.

I decided to risk the nest egg I had been saving on an idea. For some time, I had been aware of the fact that, although we were selling to leaders of fashion, garment salesmen dressed no more imaginatively than salesmen in other lines of work.

We were like advertising agencies that neglect to spend money to advertise themselves. I decided to be different.

I contracted for three suits to be made according to my own design. I told the tailor to make the coats without external pockets. I also instructed him to leave side and hip pockets off the pants; instead, I wanted large button-down pockets across the front, similar to sailors' bell-bottom trousers. In an era when other suit coats were double-breasted, I asked to have mine made into single-breasted ones. I had the lapels cut to half the width of those in vogue at the time. The notches were more distinctive and cut at a different angle than standard lapel notches.

The day I wore one of those suits was a revelation to me. What happened on my first sales call was typical of the reception I was to receive almost everywhere. The buyer became intrigued with the design of my clothes. He asked if I would mind if he brought the owner of the factory to see me. The owner took one look and called for his fashion designer. And while I stood there, holding their attention first because of the clothes and then because of the story I had to tell about my own wares, I sold more textiles in one hour than I had in the previous month.

When I entered the field of insurance at the age of twenty-three, I realized from the beginning that I would need two things if I were to achieve the degree of success I wanted: a lot of friends who would like to do business with me and a superior product to offer them. Since both of these ingredients are essential to anyone who aspires to be successful in a competitive industry, I will show how I went about getting them.

Over the years, I have tried many ways of meeting people and making them my friends. They all work. They work because people want friends. They want to be liked and admired. It's human nature. Sometimes people wear such forbidding

exteriors that it's hard to believe that underneath lies the same
need to be liked that you and I possess. But make a friendly
overture to them, and they seem almost to melt before your
eyes.

When I was a young man, ostentatious parties were an ac-
ceptable social custom and a marvelous way to meet important
people. So, I became a kind of Perle Mesta of Central Park
West. I rented a huge penthouse apartment and spent a minor
fortune decorating it. In the center of the living room, I installed a glass water fountain with 140 lights in four colors.
The walls, ceilings, and floors of the entrance foyer were
mirrored. The first miniature golf course in a Manhattan penthouse was built on the terrace overlooking the Park.

As many as a thousand guests attended my parties. These
included stars of the stage and screen, celebrities from sports
and the business world, and Broadway columnists. In one of
her columns, Dorothy Kilgallen described a party at which
Rudolph Friml was tinkling on a piano while chatting with
Victor Herbert; Gene Sarazen and Al Jolson were partners on
the miniature golf course against Leo Diegel and Joseph
Schenck; Barbara Stanwyck was dancing with Jack Dempsey
while Hannah Williams, Jack's future wife, looked on; Clara
Bow was wading in the glass fountain; Jimmy Walker and
George Jessel arrived in top hats and tails fresh from speaking
engagements; and the entire cast of the Earl Carroll Vanities
was among the guests.

It was during this period of my life that I discovered the
value of publicity as a means of keeping in touch with friends.
When the above column came out, for example, I sent reprints
not only to everyone at the party but also to all my other
clients, friends, and acquaintances. Through the years, I have
done this with everything which has been written about me—
and it would take a book simply to list the newspapers, maga-

zines, house organs, and books that have published stories about me.

When I was on my honeymoon in Honolulu, I discovered a way of meeting people that worked so well I prolonged my stay there for eighteen months. When the boat docked in Hawaii, my bride and I watched as some of the passengers were greeted by friends who lived in Hawaii. These friends brought on board beautiful orchid leis which they draped over the visitors' shoulders as they kissed them. It was such a touching ceremony that the rest of us couldn't help feeling envious.

The following morning, I was down at the docks to greet the next incoming ship from the mainland. I had two Hawaiian boys with me to help carry the flower garlands. I greeted all the debarking passengers, presented them with orchid leis, and invited them to attend a pancake breakfast at my home on the following Sunday. (I had rented Doris Duke's Honolulu residence as soon as I arrived.)

My little acts of kindness to visitors to Hawaii won me not only a great many new friends but also a plethora of favorable publicity. I soon found myself a celebrity on the island. Everyone seemed to know my name and to go out of his way to greet me.

In time, the Chamber of Commerce of Honolulu realized the value of what I was doing and began greeting all visitors as I had been doing. Today, it is a tradition. And because of my part in it, I have been made the only Life Honorary Mayor of Honolulu. I am also a Life Honorary Senator from Hawaii, and an honorary member of the Aloha Temple of Honolulu.

On another occasion, I conceived the idea of insuring movie stars against loss of their most marketable features. I arranged with Lloyd's of London to insure Jimmy Durante's nose, Harpo Marx's hands, Eddie Cantor's pop eyes, Adolph Menjou's mustache, Betty Grable's legs. The insurance coverage ranged from half a million to a million dollars.

This type of accident insurance is relatively inexpensive, and the commissions were infinitesimal. However, its publicity value both to the recipients and to me was priceless. Almost every newspaper and general circulation magazine featured the new kind of insurance mania, and my picture usually appeared with those of the celebrities. People began recognizing me on planes, buses, ships, and trains. New York cab drivers started hailing me by my first name.

Today, I use my personal table at the Four Seasons restaurant in Manhattan as a kind of office at which I perform favors for others. I eat there every day I am in town, always with two or three guests. The guests are never invited haphazardly; there's always a reason why they have been brought together.

For example, when I met Tom Carlin, the coauthor of this book, he had just moved to New York to be editor-in-chief of the Alexander Hamilton Institute. A writer, as well as an editor, he was naturally anxious to meet others in his profession. So when I first invited him to lunch, my other guests were Max Lerner of the *New York Post* and Art Sears of *The Wall Street Journal.*

Since then, I have introduced him to dozens of other well-known writers and editors, including Leonard Lyons, Ed Sullivan, and Dr. Maxwell Maltz. I also wrote a book on *Sales Management* for his company, and lined up three of my friends to write for the Institute: Julien Elfenbein, a business publications expert; Harry R. White, head of the Sales Executives Club of New York; and J. Harry Wood, president of Home Life Insurance Company.

As I have mentioned, many of the things that I do are newsworthy and get written up in various media. When this happens, I make reprints which I distribute far and wide. But even when nothing particularly newsworthy happens, I try to do something which will make the occasion memorable.

For example, when I introduced Tom Carlin to Max Lerner and Art Sears I had a photographer take a picture of us seated at my table in front of the restaurant's famous fountain. I had the picture mounted in attractive mahogany frames and sent copies to Tom, Max, and Art. Another copy hangs in my office along with several hundred of me with other guests.

Another thing that I do is collect business aphorisms which I put on calendars, calling cards, and stickers for widespread distribution. I call these Letergrams, and I find that I get a great deal of mileage out of them, mostly because they are so true that they hit home when people read them. These have been widely quoted in magazines and house organs. The following are typical of the thousands of Letergrams that I have used:

> The largest room in the world is the room for improvement.
>
> It's not the hours you put in; it's what you put in the hours.
>
> You'll never find time for anything; if you want time, you must make it.
>
> One sure way to know more about people is to know more people.
>
> The way to win friends is to be one.
>
> Luck is preparation meeting opportunity.
>
> The best way to crush your laurels is to lean on them.
>
> A man should work eight hours and sleep eight hours, but not the same eight hours.
>
> A good thing you can give and still keep is your word.
>
> An error becomes a mistake only when you refuse to correct it.

ELMER G. LETERMAN. Master salesman, author, president
of Leterman-Gortz, Inc., 1968 nominee for Horatio Alger award

COMMANDER EDWARD WHITEHEAD, C.B.E. Chairman of Schweppes (USA) Ltd., chairman of Schweppes (Canada) Ltd., chairman of L. Rose & Co. (America) Ltd.

HELEN GURLEY BROWN. Author, editor of *Cosmopolitan* magazine

THOMAS W. MATTHEW, M.D. First Negro neurosurgeon in the United States, president of NEGRO, founder and executive director of Interfaith Hospital in Queens, New York

MESHULAM RIKLIS. Chairman and president, Rapid-American Corporation

VIRGINIA GRAHAM. Author, TV star, hostess on ABC television's *Girl Talk*

MAXWELL MALTZ, M.D. Plastic surgeon, author, public speaker, founder of schools in Psycho-Cybernetics

Eugene Cook

JOHN KLUGE. Chairman and president, Metromedia, Inc., chairman and treasurer, Kluge, Finkelstein & Co.

JAMES F. O'NEIL. Publisher of *American Legion* magazine, former national commander of American Legion

DR. WENDELL PHILLIPS. Explorer, author, oil concessionaire, economic adviser to the Kingdom of Oman

JOAN CRAWFORD. Academy-Award-winning Hollywood actress, director of Pepsi-Cola Co.

D. K. Dougherty

W. CLEMENT STONE. President, Combined Insurance Company of America, chairman and president of Hawthorn Books, vice-president and director of Alberto Culver, editor and publisher of *Success Unlimited* magazine, recipient of Horatio Alger award

J. HARRY WOOD. President, Home Life Insurance Company

HARRY R. WHITE. Executive director of Sales Executives Club of New York

JOHN BODETTE. Executive vice-president of Florists' Telegraph Delivery Association

The person who never does any more than he gets paid for, never gets paid for any more than he does.

The best place to find a helping hand is at the end of your arm.

The surest way to go broke is to sit around waiting for a break.

Too many salesmen know how to say nothing; too few know when.

A man is not paid for having brains but for using them.

Beware of the man who talks of what he did instead of what he's doing.

All these activities that I have been describing are means that I use to meet people, to make them my friends, and to keep them my friends. From a business point of view, this means that I have engendered a warm climate in which a sale can more easily be made.

I hope that the reader appreciates the fact that few people buy anything as important as insurance simply on the basis of friendship. Making friends only gives a salesman a favorable hearing. To close the sale, he must have a competitive edge. In my business, a competitive edge means better product, better know-how, better experience, and better service. I have always had this advantage. For one thing, I associated myself with an outstanding partner, and for another, we represent more than thirty different insurance companies.

There is an advantage, of course, in representing many companies. Each seeks some competitive edge of its own. The more one represents, the broader his potential. Many times we have landed a king-size policy because we were able to say, "Yes, we can match that feature and then some."

Business insurance of all kinds is highly competitive; group and pension plans are especially so. Usually, a proposed group plan is let out to bids and dozens of proposals are submitted. Many of these are eliminated simply because the agents have been unable to bid on the precise specifications. In such situations, we can usually come closer to matching what a company wants or needs than agents who must limit their proposals to the type of coverage underwritten by a single company. Very often we can bring to bear creative thinking, triggered by our broad knowledge of the field, to find a solution that no one else has thought of.

But my real edge comes from the organization behind me. For client-oriented service is the real key to keeping business insurance in force. Over the years, I have been fortunate in having as my partner one of the most knowledgeable men in the business. I really need this kind of support because, as I have indicated, my forte is to make friends, which is only half the battle. I had this in mind twenty years ago when I persuaded my present partner, Norman Gortz, to join forces with me. "Norman," I said, "I can open doors for you, but the rest is up to you. You'll have to follow through from the original introduction to the sale."

At the time, Norman was a fast-rising young executive in the group department of the John Hancock Mutual Life Insurance Company. He held the position of regional sales manager for greater New York. He was a Chartered Life Underwriter, and people were already saying that he knew more about group insurance than anyone else in the business. A high honor student throughout his schooling, Norman has the most brilliant mind of anyone I have met in my half century in business.

In the twenty years that we have been associated, Norman has continued to steep himself in the complexities of insurance, especially group plans. He is the outstanding expert in our field of operations. Not satisfied with this distinction, he has, by studying five nights a week for three years, added a law degree to his other educational credits.

But most important of all, Norman has followed through. He has built an organization that provides faster and more expert group service than any in the country. Our men are trained to underwrite the plans we bid on, compare and compete among companies, prepare the employee announcement booklets, supervise the installation, set up the administrative systems and procedures, and extend a continuing service that solves problems as they arise and keeps the group plans running smoothly.

So you see, I do not concern myself with the details of the business. I don't have to. I leave these to Norman. I concentrate on making and keeping friends. And at some time in our relationship, many of my friends bring up the question of insurance. Whatever they ask, I tell them that I will have my partner, Norman Gortz, call them. Norman follows through.

Has the operation been a success? It has indeed. For over forty years, I have been lucky enough to break records in almost every facet of insurance sales. During the eighteen months I was in Hawaii, for example, my sales of insurance were in the millions, and this was during the great depression. *Forbes* magazine rates me as one of the twelve master salesmen in the world. *Insurance* magazine writes that I should be recognized as the first and only member of the BDRT (Billion Dollar Round Table). The magazine points out that I have personally sold more ordinary life and group insurance than 94 percent of U. S. insurance companies have in force—and many of these companies are over one hundred years old and have one thousand full-time sales representatives. These are among the reasons, perhaps, that I was a 1968 nominee for the Horatio Alger Award along with Bob Hope and Arthur Goldberg.

But I don't measure my success by the trophies or plaques I

have won, or by the size of the bank account it all has given me. And I don't measure it by seventeen bulging scrapbooks lying around my home and office. I measure it by the quality and duration of the friendships that I have made. And in this respect, I'll match my life with any man's.

Commander
Edward Whitehead, C.B.E.

Commander Edward Whitehead's precise British accent and bristling reddish-brown beard are as familiar to millions of Americans as the tangy Schweppes products that he promotes. But what is not so generally known is the scope of his influence over the whole Schweppes operation in this country, in Canada, and in Latin America north of the equator.

Besides acting as a director of the parent company in England, the Commander is chairman of Schweppes (USA) Ltd., chairman of Schweppes (Canada) Ltd., and chairman of L. Rose & Co. (America) Ltd. (lime juice and preserves). He is responsible for the entire operation in these areas. And since he first stepped off a transatlantic plane in January, 1953, to establish his headquarters in New York City, his master plan for marketing Schweppes in the new world has resulted in a 2,000 percent increase in sales.

The Schweppes products, of course, are not new. The parent company in London is the oldest manufacturer of artificial mineral water in existence. In 1794, it began to produce soda, classified then as a patent medicine. The Commander says that innumerable customers still claim benefit from his company's tonic water, but so far as he knows it does them no good whatsoever. "However," he adds, "it does them no harm and it is a pleasant drink—curiously refreshing!"

17

During the first half of the nineteenth century, British subjects serving their country overseas, especially in India, were encouraged to take daily doses of quinine to ward off malaria. In order to improve the unappetizing taste of neat quinine, Schweppes made its now famous tonic water containing quinine and mixed it in gin. Gradually, a large class of people grew to enjoy the tang of quinine in their gin. Schweppes tonic water achieved instant popularity in India as well as in Britain and other countries of the world.

When Commander Whitehead joined the organization to learn the business as advertising manager in 1950, Schweppes products were recognized by discriminating consumers the world over as superior mixers. For over one and a half centuries, the company's objective had been to project a quality image. The best people drank Schweppes, and the best places sold it. In effect, the business had been run by gentlemen for gentlemen, and the company was happy with its small but faithful market.

The fact that a product which was sold to a limited market has been able to retain its quality image when it is now sold to a broad general market stands as a tribute to the ingenious marketing techniques used by the Schweppes management, and in the North American market by Commander Whitehead. Some of the credit for this achievement must be attributed to the Commander's appearance in the Schweppes advertising, an idea suggested by another remarkable Briton who has gained fame in the new world, David Ogilvy.

The Commander is so obviously a gentleman that his very presence in the ads plants the unexpressed idea that the Schweppes products are the aristocrats of their class. And for soft drinks that sell for about sixteen cents a bottle, this sort of reputation represents an incredible publicity achievement.

The Commander recognizes the value of his appearing in

Schweppes advertising. But he has never been happy with this particular role. He does not consider himself an actor, and he detests the days he has to spend posing for the commercials. However, he insists that the ads show him engaged in activities that he actually does in real life. Another consoling factor is the fact that he will soon be phased out of the ads. Although the company's advertising has maintained continuity for fifteen years, Schweppes management, including the Commander, recognizes the need to bring this phase to an end voluntarily. As the Commander puts it, "The risks are too great. Primarily because of the unwisdom of placing all your goodwill eggs in one so vulnerable basket, not to mention the wear and tear on the individual."

As important as the Schweppes ads have been, they represent only a small part of the overall strategy that has made Schweppes a household word on the North American continent. For the Commander's real genius lies in marketing.

"Marketing," as he explains it, "is a creative process. It embodies research and development—finding new products and new uses for existing products. The creative approach is no less vital in product design, package design, presentation, promotion, publicity, advertising, and point of sale—all these things are facets of the marketing plan, as are channels of distribution and the recruitment, training, and incentive of the sales force."

His knowledge of American marketing methods—"learned while doing," as he puts it, and adapted to British needs—has brought about a revolution in what might be regarded as Schweppes' traditional approach.

Perhaps the most drastic change has been in price. When the Commander assumed the presidency of Schweppes (USA) Ltd., the retail price of Schweppes tonic was sixty cents a bottle. This high cost made the product prohibitive to all except the lucky minority who never bother to consider cost when buying. By importing the essence only, adding the water (treated to Schweppes' exacting specifications) and the Schweppervescence here, the Commander was able, with no sacrifice of quality, to reduce the retail price to sixteen cents a bottle. For the first time, Schweppes was made available at a price to fit the pocketbook of the average new-world consumer.

Another radical change was in the company's method of getting intensive local distribution. The Commander achieved this by establishing franchised territories and encouraging the local bottler to use his access to the market and knowledge of local conditions to Schweppes' and the bottler's advantage.

His franchise operations have been resoundingly successful due in part to his careful selection of franchisers. His basic criterion is to pick only persons who can be relied on to "uphold the high standards that Schweppes has always maintained." He is determined that the management and sales staff of his bottlers and distributors in North America "will never do or say anything in the conduct of their business that they would be ashamed of doing personally."

But this is only the beginning. He also believes that the men on the firing line must be given vigorous support. One facet of this is the national advertising already mentioned. Another is the publicity and public relations thrust provided by the creative activities of the Commander. In this respect, he is one of the most active men I know.

On a typical tour last year, for example, Commander Whitehead started by making a trip to New Orleans to help launch the operations of a new bottler, Louis Freeman. While there, he presented a Schweppes trophy at the Southern Yacht Club, made what he referred to as "the usual round of interviews and speeches," and was entertained, along with his public relations director, Lord Francis Newall, aboard the yacht of a director on the board of the parent company of Coca-Cola Company (Atlanta).

He then spent two days in Philadelphia, where he made a speech to four hundred Rotarians, gave a number of interviews, and threw a party for Inez and Manny Lowenstein and their Booth Bottling Company's managers and salesmen.

Two days later, he was in southern California where he attended a reception at Statham House, Los Angeles' official hospitality center; gave a dinner party for Peter Sellers and his wife, Britt Eklund; and acted as guest interviewer for a Los Angeles television station, where he talked with Dr. Nelson Glueck, an archaeologist and authority on the Middle East; from this interview, he rushed to the opening of Senor Pico's at Century Plaza, a new Mexican restaurant started by his friend Victor Bergeron, who owns the Trader Vic's chain of restaurants; plus, of course, the usual round of interviews and speeches.

The Commander consciously tries to direct any publicity he receives while on these junkets to promote and support local bottlers. As time goes on, this becomes relatively easier for him to do, since he is now a kind of living symbol for Schweppes.

Each of the other aspects of marketing are also accorded their rightful place in the Schweppes scheme of things. This adds up to a perfectly blended marketing mix. The Commander's direct-mail campaigns, for example, help bolster the somewhat snobbish appeal which naturally goes along with an imported British product. When he tested Bitter Lemon in the American marketplace, he wrote letters from England, on English writing paper, and sent these full rate with English stamps to a "peer group" in the test market.

The letter described Bitter Lemon, its uses, and explained how the recipient could sample the product at Schweppes' expense. The results, carefully checked, revealed that repeat business was coming from the parts of town where the peer group resided. As a result, personal letters to peer groups in other cities followed. The fact that influential persons were buying the product then helped salesmen convince store buyers to carry supplies of Schweppes' Bitter Lemon.

Another aspect of the Commander's marketing strategy is his use of depth research. This provides him with guidelines on such matters as the existence and extent of the overall market, the share he commands of it, the attitudes of the public toward his products, alternative channels of distribution, and the like. No one is more aware than he is of the need to keep one's fingers on the pulse of a market. He realizes that change is of the nature of things. A successful company stays successful only so long as it stands ready to gear its marketing to the changing attitudes and tastes of the fickle consuming public.

A recent study shows that most people who drink quinine water are resolutely convinced that Schweppes is the best and represents top quality. Even people who do not drink such products have a similarly strong impression. Such acceptance is singular proof of the effectiveness of the marketing techniques employed by the Commander, aided, he insists, by a first-class staff.

All this has not been easy for an Englishman operating in an alien business climate, for before he took over U. S. operations, the Commander had little experience with business outside of England. His first job, after he graduated from local schools in Hampshire in southern England, was in the General Assurance Company, a leading British company. After World War II, during which he rose to the rank of Commander in Her Majesty's Navy, he became head of a foundation devoted to raising scholastic and training levels in British industry.

Then, he served as a troubleshooter in industrial relations under Sir Stafford Cripps, Chancellor of the Exchequer.

When he came here, the Commander had to adapt to American attitudes and practices that differ radically from those of his countrymen. The English have a tendency to resist salesmen. They have a natural reticence and abhor the vigorous and positive approach that successful salesmen take in this country. The Commander preferred our more direct approach, for Americans as a group like and expect to be sold. If the salesman does not try hard, we are inclined to suspect that something is wrong with the goods. We react negatively to a salesman who gives the impression that he is holding back, or, as the Commander puts it, "keeping one foot on dry land, so to speak."

In order to grapple successfully in the American market-place, the Commander chose to adopt our methods. He steeped himself in this country's practices and techniques. He was so thorough in his homework that he has become an expert on the subject of importing goods and marketing them to American consumers. He was made chairman of the British Export Marketing Advisory Committee, appointed by the British National Export Council Committee for Exports to the U.S.A. His friend David Ogilvy is deputy chairman. Among the other members are Marvin Bower, managing director of McKinsey & Co., Inc.; Professor Edward Bursk, editor of the *Harvard Business Review;* Sir John Chadwick, K.C.M.G., Minister, British Embassy, Washington, D. C.; and General James Gavin, chairman of Arthur D. Little, Inc.

In 1966, the British Export Marketing Advisory Committee issued a booklet entitled "Marketing in the U.S.A." In 1967, BEMAC, under the direction of the Commander, issued the "BEMAC Report," a detailed blueprint of the market opportunities and marketing action that British importers should follow in gaining a foothold in the United States.

We have seen that there are many reasons which combine to explain the success of Schweppes (USA) Ltd.: the company's creative and discursive approach to marketing, ingenious advertising, sustained favorable publicity, superior direct-mail pieces, and, most important, happy and effective relations with bottlers and distributors. But if one were to look for a root cause for the success of Schweppes in North America, it would have to be attributed to the philosophy which has guided the Commander in all his actions. For he often says that "a run-of-the-mill approach brings run-of-the-mill results, whereas an inspired approach brings inspired results."

Although he still retains a country cottage on Chichester Harbour in England, Commander Whitehead and his family have maintained residency in the United States since he took over the Schweppes operation in North America. He has recently given up his apartment in Manhattan in order to spend more time in a house of his own design in Connecticut and a ski lodge in Vermont. Very soon, his office is moving to Stamford, Connecticut, where most of his executives already have homes.

I would be remiss and painting a one-dimensional picture of him if I were to leave the impression that the Commander is all work and no play. He skis most winter weekends in Vermont, and in past years has spent the Easter holidays with his family at Val d'Isère in southern France. He swims almost every day. In fact, he likes swimming so much that he built an indoor pool in his new Connecticut home. He also enjoys fox hunting, beagling, and sailing. He keeps meticulously fit with morning exercises. He rarely smokes and, when he does, it is either a cigar or pipe. In keeping with his love of outdoor activities, he is such a fast walker that most of his companions are hard put to keep up with him. His beard is graying now, but he still looks ten years younger than one would expect of a grandfather three times over.

The Commander is also somewhat of an explorer. In the fifteen years that he has been in this country, he has traveled widely, and knows the United States better than most Americans. He especially likes to get off the beaten trails. He waxes enthusiastic about the wonders of our natural heritage, our national parks, and our mountains, rivers, and lakes.

As with his Schweppes products, there is something curiously refreshing about Commander Whitehead, the man. He throws himself enthusiastically into his work, never holding back and never falling into complacent routines. And yet he admits freely that the Schweppes products are hardly of earthshaking importance in the bigger scheme of things. As he sees them, they simply represent one of the amenities of life. He drinks them "nature" in the daytime. But he sees nothing wrong in adding liquor since, as he says, the human ego is soluble in alcohol.

Curiously refreshing.

Helen Gurley Brown

It would be obvious to say that Helen Gurley Brown has dared to be different because she has taken the hush out of sex for the working girl. And Helen deserves a weightier assessment. She has done more than unwrap some of the glamorous aspects of extra-curricular lovemaking. She has dared to dignify the life of the career girl, whether in or out of bed.

The essence of her philosophy is that a working girl can have the best of two worlds; married or not, she can enjoy the choice compensations of marital as well as single life. To do so, however, she must be willing to let out all the stops in the pursuit of excellence. For there's no particular glamour in being marooned in a typing pool or hidden away among the file cabinets. The glamour is in the front office where the action is, and where, says Helen, the prime specimens of American manhood lurk.

To get to the front office on more than a temporary visa, a girl must work very hard. But the compensations are worth it. The working girl who is up front where it counts makes enough money to mold herself into a glamour puss and generally travel first class. What's more, she's surrounded by attractive, well-groomed, well-heeled intelligent males for more hours a day than the most pampered nonworking married woman.

Helen's message and advice are based on a wealth of experience. Her own. She has been a working girl all of her adult life, and she remained single until she was thirty-seven years old. When she did marry, she succumbed to a highly eligible forty-four-year-old motion picture producer. But a successful marriage is not surprising for Helen; she has always been successful. Her life stands as a living testimonial to the soundness of the advice she dispenses.

Even as a young girl in her home state of Arkansas, where her father was in the state legislature in Little Rock, Helen had what she calls compulsive work habits. In grade school, she used to write stories and poems and turn them in to astonished teachers who had not asked for them. She also put on a great many programs in the auditorium. She would sing, dance, play the piano, or work up some kind of original skit. These were not assigned tasks. She volunteered.

When she was eleven, Helen and a girl friend started giving dancing lessons in the friend's house in Little Rock. This was in 1933, the depths of the depression. In retrospect, Helen is still amazed to think that they were successful in getting children to pay for lessons in that dismal year.

When her father died, the family moved to California and Helen entered Los Angeles' John H. Francis Polytechnic High School. "I was always in the thick of things. Every year, I was either running for office, or I held some office. But I did manage to graduate as class valedictorian."

What makes Helen run? She isn't sure. But like many successful people, she's intensely interested in "drive." Even as an eight-year-old, she was competitive. On one occasion she worked for a week on a Bible-story booklet in order to compete for an announced prize in Sunday school. She won by default. No one else had an entry.

"Perhaps it was because I felt I was underprivileged. It

may have been heightened by the death of my father when I
was ten. At that tender age I started to worry about money
although he left us some insurance. In high school, I know that
I was partly motivated because of a terrible case of acne. You
don't see acne anymore like it was in the 1930's and 1940's.
Doctors must know a lot more about it and its prevention. Just
at the time that you are at the height of insecurity, these
bumps come out. Unconsciously, you know that if you are
going to be noticed or liked at all, you have to do something
extra. I just felt that I had to be bubbly and charming and
carry on and be pleasant to be with and generally wonderful!"

After one semester in college ("the English professor asked
for a short biographical sketch, and I turned in thirty-five
pages"), the financial situation at home became more critical.
Helen's sister contracted polio. Her mother had to postpone
going back to a teaching career to care for the stricken girl.
Helen entered a business school where she took courses in
typing and shorthand while holding down a part-time six-
dollars-a-week job. The job was to tabulate the mail for a
morning show on radio station KHJ in Hollywood. "I was a
little tyke of eighteen—flat-chested, pale, acne-skinned, terri-
fied, and convinced of one thing only: Working in an office
was practically the most gruesome thing that could happen to
a woman."

She worked her way through seventeen jobs in half that
number of years. "I changed jobs mostly for more money.
Girls don't seem to care about money as much today. Perhaps
it's because everyone is more affluent." After leaving the radio
station, Helen worked for the Beverly Hills headquarters of
Music Corporation of America, which at the time represented
top Hollywood stars like Paulette Goddard, Dick Powell, and
Joan Crawford. Her next stint was for Eddie Cantor's gag
writers. Then she moved on to work for Abbott and Costello's

radio show. In quick succession, she worked for Jack Carson, Frank Buck, the William Morris Agency, and the Los Angeles *Daily News.* She took a job as secretary for Howard Hawks's brother Bill who was writing a book but who never once asked her to take a word of dictation. ("He did have the most fascinating callers though.") She became secretary to a wealthy builder who, it turned out, hated Communists, Catholics, Roosevelt, but most of all Jews. This job lasted only until the builder discovered to his horror that Helen's roommate was Jewish.

When she was twenty-five, Helen finally landed an honest-to-God "front office" position as executive secretary to Don Belding, board chairman of Foote, Cone and Belding advertising agency. By then, she was ready not only for the responsibilities of a demanding job but also for the fun and excitement that go with it.

Helen's mother and sister had returned to Arkansas a year earlier. Her mother resumed her career as a teacher. "Mother taught school until she was forcibly retired at age seventy! She misses it very much because she is a career girl herself, which is probably how I got stung by the bug. Mother has always been a strong believer in women developing their talents. She went back to college to get some additional teaching credits when she was sixty-two."

Helen's sister is still in a wheelchair as a result of polio; however, she's happily married to a man she met in a rehabilitation center for war veterans. They reside in Oklahoma.

So besides having a job where people like Jack Dempsey, General Omar Bradley, and even Howard Hughes dropped in, Helen was now living in her own apartment in Los Angeles. Without knowing it, she was starting to accumulate the fund of knowledge that she would someday translate into sensational but sound advice on living alone, and sundry items of interest to the career girl.

Through the years, Helen continued to produce unassigned writing projects. When Don Belding was out of town, which was often, she spent the greater part of her working day writing long, gossipy letters to him. Both he and his wife enjoyed her breezy style but, except for one copywriting project the agency gave her, nothing resulted from these letters for several years. Then one day, she entered a contest in *Glamour* magazine. For her, the contest was therapy for a romance that had gone awry. One of the questions to be answered was, "What is your ambition?" She had no interest in being anything except Mr. Belding's executive secretary, but knew that this answer would hardly win points in a contest. So, she wrote that she wanted to be a copywriter. When the magazine printed her answer, the boss took her at her printed word, gave her an office and an account to work on.

As a copywriter, Helen came into her own. Her natural talent as a wordsmith was quickly forged into a craft by the creative demands of her work. Cleveland Amory says that she is incapable of writing a dull sentence. Helen says that the only effective writing education she has undergone was in writing copy. She had taken two extension courses at UCLA and liked them. "But I never got a glimmer that I had talent. They didn't read even one paper of mine in class. And, as usual, I turned in a lot more than they assigned."

Perhaps the main reason that she was a successful copywriter stems from the fact that she has such an abiding respect for the profession. "When people spend $100,000 for a two-page color spread, and you have only three short paragraphs to write, they better be good. They better not bore anybody, and they better get the message across. The headline must grab the reader. You can't afford to babble on and on or say anything dumb."

Following the formula that she advocates for someone who has found her niche in business, Helen let out all the stops when she became a copywriter. She rose rapidly. Within a few years, other agencies were stalking her. But she stayed with Foote, Cone and Belding for ten years, moving to Kenyon & Eckhardt for a salary twice the one she was making. Within a short time, she was the highest paid advertising woman on the West Coast.

In 1959, Helen married David Brown, vice-president and director of story operations for Twentieth Century–Fox. David himself has a fascinating background in writing and publishing. He has held such positions as editor of *Liberty* magazine, editorial director for the American Medical Association, managing editor for *Cosmopolitan,* and editorial vice-president for New American Library. Along the way, he wrote jokes for Eddie Cantor, turned out horoscopes for vending machines, sold stories to *Reader's Digest, Harper's,* and *Saturday Evening Post.*

For three years, Helen enjoyed the heady atmosphere of being tops in her field. Then she fell out of favor with the eighth of Kenyon & Eckhardt's nine successive creative directors. For a time, she was miserable. "I was the same girl with the same talents I had before. If they asked for nine ideas, I would come up with sixty-two. But nothing I did could melt the icicles."

But out of adversity often spring life's most interesting surprises. At David's suggestion, she decided to sublimate her professional unhappiness by writing a book. David suggested the content and the title: *Sex and the Single Girl.* The book was a runaway best seller that has been published in twenty-eight countries and translated into sixteen languages.

Many people are attracted to *Sex and the Single Girl* because of its provocative title. But once they start reading, they discover to their delight and edification that it's an interesting and informative work. It is honest, thoughtful, and upbeat from beginning to end. Its message is that single girls should stop fretting about finding a husband. They are not creatures to be pitied and patronized. They are living in a "far more colorful world than the one of P.T.A., Dr. Spock, and the jammed clothes dryer." The book reflects the talent of a first-class writer. It has personality, charm, and sparkling wit.

What it doesn't have is any trace of the pornographic approach to sex that is so common in current literature—and so sophomoric! "Sex is more than the act of coitus. It begins with the delicious feeling of attraction between two people. It may never go further, but sex it is. And a single woman may promote the attraction, bask in the sensation, drink it like wine, and pour it over her like blossoms, with never a guilty twinge."

Most of *Sex and the Single Girl* is devoted to dispensing advice on how a single girl should go about attracting swarms of men and how she should then capitalize on this situation.

You can't harbor an ounce of baby fat. It never looked good on anybody but babies. When I married, I moved in with six-pound dumbbells, slant board, an electronic device for erasing wrinkles ... and enough high-powered vitamins to generate life in a statue.

You must develop style. Every girl has one ... it's just a case of getting it out in the open, caring for it and feeding it like an orchid until it leafs out.

Roommates are for sorority girls. You need an apartment alone even if it's over a garage.

The overwhelming response to *Sex and the Single Girl* convinced Helen Gurley Brown that she had unearthed a winning formula. She quit her job and began answering her mail through a syndicated newspaper column called "Woman Alone." The column remained faithful to the theme of her book. Helen wrote more fully on subjects such as careers, apartments, diets, clothes, and beauty. Later, she converted many of the ideas from these columns into a book, *Helen Gurley Brown's Outrageous Opinions.*

While writing the syndicated column, she began another book, *Sex and the Office.* This proved to be a brilliant sequel to the first. "I wanted to write about girls in offices—how wonderful they are and how their office life can be rewarding, sexy, and exciting."

Meanwhile, Helen was engaged in other pursuits. ("I feel that the only way I get the best out of me is to be hopelessly overextended.") To promote her books, she appeared on several hundred network and local programs in the United States, Canada, and Europe, including the "Today," "Tonight," and "What's My Line" shows. She started recording for Crescendo Records, also accepted public-speaking engagements before professional, university, church, and civic groups.

In the spring of 1964, Helen and David Brown decided there ought to be a magazine slanted at her hip audience of single and working girls, and they worked up a prospectus for such a magazine to be called *Femme.* Publishers, however, shied away because the cost of getting such a venture off the launching pad would be astronomical. Finally, Bernard Geis, Helen's publisher, presented the idea to Richard Deems, the president of Hearst publications. In March, 1965, Mr. Deems offered Helen the editorship of *Cosmopolitan* magazine. She accepted.

Cosmopolitan was foundering. Advertising revenue was down 20 percent from the previous year. The magazine, sold almost entirely over newsstands which means that it could not depend on subscriptions supporting it, was rapidly losing circulation volume. Helen immediately set about reorienting the editorial focus of *Cosmopolitan* to fit her successful formula. She canceled stories, paid off writers and photographers working on assignments, and farmed out new assignments slanted to an entirely new market.

"The magazine is now aimed less toward the family and more toward the modern young woman. She can have a husband and children, but she doesn't live through them. We treat her as her own person, very involved in life. We want pieces that tell a hip, attractive, 18- to 34-year-old, good-citizen girl how to have a more rewarding life. We're interested in articles on careers, part-time jobs, diets, foods, fashion, men, the entertainment world, emotions, money, medicine, and fabulous characters. We're female oriented but expect to have men eavesdropping as women do in *Playboy* and *Esquire.*"

Within a few months, the results of her efforts had the magazine industry agog. *Cosmo* began to be a success. Although the editorial budget was not increased and the magazine continued to be sold almost exclusively from newsstands, sales zoomed as high as 1 million copies per issue. What made this so extraordinary was the fact that practically the entire readership switched. The new readers come from the ranks of single girls and married working girls.

How is *Cosmo* doing now that the furor has died down, and the month-to-month drudgery of putting a magazine to bed has set in? Let's first look at the obstacles to success. Hearst has increased Helen's editorial budget per issue by only $2,000. It has not chosen to go after subscribers as this is not necessarily the way to profits.

"Ninety-seven percent of our sales come from newsstands. We do offer a twelve-month subscription for five dollars, a savings of a dollar. But that's as far as we will go. You know that a fifty-cent magazine can buy all the subscriptions it wants for seven cents a copy. *Life* magazine bought subscriptions when *Look*'s circulation threatened to pass *Life*'s. But this proved so expensive *Life* finally let *Look* pass, and the world didn't end. It's not circulation but profit that counts."

In spite of a fairly stabilized budget, Helen has created a profitable enterprise. ("The Hearst people have given me wonderful freedom to use my own editorial judgment.") Sales have increased 16 percent since Helen took over. The magazine now guarantees advertisers monthly sales of 961,000 copies, as opposed to 800,000 when Helen came in (they were actually considerably below that), and it delivers this figure. What's more important, advertising revenue doubled to $3 million. "The new *Cosmo* is strictly for 18- to 34-year-olds. From the advertisers' point of view, the format is on target as a magazine ought to be. We now can show certain kinds of advertisers—cosmetics, fashion, travel, liquor—that our readers will buy their products."

To keep the demand soaring, Helen writes the cover blurbs for *Cosmopolitan* (the trickiest and most important element in the sale of a magazine bought on impulse), and also writes an inside column and does considerable editing herself.

As if this were not enough to keep her busy, she takes on other jobs. She is supervising editor of *Eye*, the new Hearst teen-age magazine. She also has a syndicated, five-days-a-week television show, *Outrageous Opinions*. In addition, she manages to set aside a few hours a week to write. She has a new book coming out this fall, *The Helen Gurley Brown Single Girl Cookbook*.

Since Helen married David Brown, she has become a celebrity. She is recognized everywhere she goes. Does her husband resent this? "David feels that he invented me. And it's true. He has been able to get creativity out of me that I didn't know I had. Moreover, he's involved in everything I do.

He's my mentor, my guru. He edits my work, and is a superb editor as well as a writer. He sometimes helps me write the blurbs for *Cosmo*. It was his idea that I write the newspaper column. And he likes my making money. He didn't marry me for it. In fact, he didn't think that I should keep working. But since I work, he thinks it's marvelous that I'm successful."

What happens in the private life of a woman if she writes and talks as freely about sex as Helen does? Do wives worry about their husbands when she's around? Do men make more passes? Does she receive hate mail?

"I don't have any more problems with wives or their husbands than the next girl. The thing is, my writing and talking about sex is never gamy or provocative. Also, I was thirty-nine when I started writing the book, forty when it came out. I'm now forty-six. I'm too mature for men to come up and pinch me and say, 'Let's go to a motel.' I'm also not the type. As for hate mail, I'm sure there is some of it, but I don't see it. Someone else scans my mail, and removes it. It doesn't help to read it. It's never very constructive."

When she looks to the future, Helen sees more of the same kind of activities for herself. She revels in her job with *Cosmopolitan*, but she also realizes that each year will remove her just a little more from the empathy she has with her audience of 18- to 34-year-olds. However, she knows that she will continue to write. "Perhaps someday, I'll feel I've had it with business, and I will do something philanthropic. Really give my soul to it. It may be something for the Negro movement—but I hope that's solved by then. But I know one thing. I will be busy. I will never be at home lounging around."

Thomas W. Matthew, M.D.

$\mathbf{D}$r. Thomas W. Matthew is the only Negro leader involved in civil-rights work who achieved prominence and success outside of the civil rights movement. He sacrificed an affluent life to do something for the betterment of his race.

Dr. Matthew dares to be different in many ways. During his high-income years when he was practicing neurosurgery full time, he did not file Federal income tax returns. He says that he eventually intends to pay the government the money he owes but not until his "patient" is cured. Dr. Matthew's patient is the Negro community where, with the money withheld from taxes, he has established fifteen self-help industries including a hospital and a construction company.

Dr. Matthew's solution to the so-called Negro problem is self-help. He scorns handouts from any source and has steadfastly refused charity when offered to his organization NEGRO (National Economic Growth and Reconstruction Organization). Almost single-handedly he has proved that his program is workable in and applicable to all Negro ghettos across the nation. And in spite of monumental obstacles, he has so far kept the faith with those who believe in him. As president of NEGRO, he has not made promises that he has been unable to deliver. Whether he can continue is a moot question. He faces mounting pressures because of his almost total indifference to governmental authority when its aims conflict with his own.

By any standards, Dr. Matthew is a remarkable man. From the humblest of beginnings (his father was a janitor and for a while was on welfare), he rose to become the first Negro neurosurgeon trained in the United States. He was outstanding as a student, usually as the only Negro in all-white schools. He was the founder of Interfaith Hospital in Queens, the first new hospital established in New York for over forty years. As president of NEGRO, which receives no government or foundation grants and is supported entirely by earnings and the sale of 6½ percent bonds, he operates a complex of companies that provides jobs, trains and rehabilitates hard-core Negro unemployables, such as drug addicts and unwed mothers.

In order to understand the motivations of this complex man and the magnitude of what he has already accomplished, one has to go back to see how he got where he is today.

Tom Matthew was born in New York, one of eight children. He was eighteen years old before he lived outside of an apartment house basement. During part of Tom's childhood, the family was on welfare because his father lost a leg in an accident. "The best part of our day was going through the dumbwaiter looking for goodies discarded by tenants."

Since his father worked in all-white apartment buildings in white neighborhoods, Tom, until he went to medical school in the South, attended predominantly white schools. He was an exceptional student. At the Bronx High School of Science, he graduated with honors and was elected president of the student body for two consecutive years. He was on the school's basketball team and was an honor student.

When he attended Manhattan College, he was the only Negro in the school. The alumni association furnished him with a scholarship as the first Negro to attend Manhattan. He earned straight A's for the first three years. In his last year he worked as superintendent of ten apartment buildings but still managed to stay on the dean's list.

In spite of this apparent academic and social success in white schools, Dr. Matthew does not look back with fond nostalgia on this period of his life. In fact, his memories are so painful that he does not want to subject his own children to similar experiences; all five of them attend public schools in Harlem. "I was a showcase Negro and encountered much duplicity and hypocrisy on the part of students and teachers. I think the experience hurt my personality. I would have many more friends today if I had gone to school with Negroes. The whites all proved to be temporary friends."

When asked, Dr. Matthew can cite many examples of treatment that made him feel uncomfortable in white schools. In the third grade, when the class was reading the story of Little Black Sambo, the teacher pointed to him and said, "Just like Tommy." On another occasion, the class was reading about the Little Black Imp that jumped out of a box. The teacher said, "Stand up Tom so the class can see what a Little Black Imp looks like."

"Many of the things that happened convinced me that basic changes must be made in our socioeconomic system before whites and Negroes can hope to integrate properly. One time, for example, I was invited to the home of one of my classmates. He made me hide in the closet when his father came home from work earlier than expected. I was hurt and angered by this incident."

At Meharry Medical College in Nashville, Tennessee, he made the dean's list each year as an honor student. He was awarded the Assistant Laboratory Instructorship in histology and neuroanatomy at the end of his first year. He completed his studies with high academic awards and as a member of the Medical Honor Society.

While he was an intern at St. Louis City Hospital, Dr. Matthew for the first time came face to face with the defeatist attitude that many Negroes adopt—they reach the point where they do not believe that the better things in life are possible for them to achieve. One day, Dr. Matthew, who had confidently been telling anyone who asked that he planned to be a neurosurgeon, entered the hospital cafeteria where about five hundred people were eating, including the staff of the hospital. When the chief resident, a Negro, saw him, he stood up and began a chant: "There's our neu-ro-surg-eon!" A roar went up from the diners and soon the whole place was chanting, "There's our neu-ro-surg-eon! There's our neu-ro-surg-eon! There's our neu-ro-surg-eon!" Then, as the chant subsided, the resident surgeon cupped his hands around his mouth and shouted: "What makes you think that you're going to make it, nigger?"

It wasn't easy for Dr. Matthew to make it.

When he finished his internship, he was accepted to the residency training program in surgery at the Cleveland City Hospital. As a resident he was paid fifty dollars a month which was the first money he had earned since starting medical school. Fortunately, his early training as a handyman around apartment houses equipped him to be a jack-of-all-trades. Working in the hospital machine shop in his spare time, he put together an automobile entirely from spare parts. But his hopes to be a neurosurgeon suffered a setback. When he presented himself to the surgeon at the hospital, this white doctor told him bluntly, "I won't train a colored man to be a neurosurgeon."

But his supervisor at the St. Louis City Hospital had recommended him to Harvard and on New Year's Eve in 1951, Dr. Matthew received a phone call inviting him to take a position at the Harvard Medical Center in Boston. He was told that, if he accepted, he would have to be in Boston the next day. He borrowed fifty dollars from a Negro physician who was at the New Year's Eve party, packed his meager belongings in his homemade automobile, and departed within the hour.

At Harvard Medical Center, Dr. Matthew received training in neurology and neurosurgery. His postgraduate work included neuropathology at the Mallory Institute of Pathology in Boston and traumatic neurosurgery at Boston City Hospital. He quickly became so skillful at neurosurgery that he was appointed chief resident physician in brain surgery at the Boston Veterans Administration Hospital and also clinical instructor of the Harvard and Boston University medical students.

He was recipient of the Dozian Fellowship award, and he moved to New York City where he became a member of Mt. Sinai Hospital's department of neurology and there conducted research on the physiology of the brain. He was also appointed to the staff of the Bronx Municipal Hospital and became clinical instructor in the Albert Einstein Medical College. In addition, he established and became director of a neurosurgery department at Coney Island Hospital.

In 1964, he took the first of several steps which have led him to give up most of his lucrative practice as a neurosurgeon and to devote full time to NEGRO. He established the Interfaith Hospital in Queens and became its executive director.

The story of Interfaith Hospital is the saga of a monumental struggle of a Negro to gain permission to act responsibly for the good of a community. At root, the troubles Dr. Matthew encountered were caused because society is not accustomed to having a Negro volunteer to carry through a major project. The authorities were shocked when Dr. Matthew applied for permission to open a new hospital. He was told by the Board of Social Welfare that his application could not be processed unless he had $100,000 cash in the bank, possession of a building, and proof of public need for another hospital in Queens.

In thirty days, Dr. Matthew had met all the conditions imposed by the Board. But when the Board examined the building that he had purchased, he was told that it would take $1 million to rehabilitate it. Dr. Matthew with the aid of 528 volunteer workers completed the job for $50,000. He himself installed the new plumbing for the third-floor operating room.

After the hospital opened, Blue Cross took six months to recognize it. Dr. Matthew had to meet his payroll and care for patients with money out of his own pocket. He was forced to borrow funds from loan sharks. He nursed the hospital through crisis after crisis, including an attempted eviction for nonpayment of a bank loan. At one point, he built and manned a barricade around the hospital to hold off city marshals who threatened to enter and evacuate the patients.

The hospital, which is now well established, marks a turning point in Dr. Matthew's life. It changed his thinking in regard to the direction that civil-rights activities should take. Before, he had been involved in the typical activities that one has come to associate with civil rights: sit-ins, picketing, and demonstrations.

At the age of thirteen, he was a representative from the Bronx at the American Youth Congress. He was elected because he was the brightest student in his class. This gave him the opportunity to have tea on the White House lawn with Mrs. Roosevelt. But it also gave him, as the only Negro on the trip, another insight into what it meant to be a Negro. On the trip to Washington, D. C., he couldn't get served in restaurants along the highway. His companions had to bring food out to him.

From age fourteen through sixteen, he was president of the Bronx Youth Division of the National Association for the Advancement of Colored People. At age fifteen, he organized a group of friends and cleared off a vacant lot for a playground, because as a Negro he was restricted from the use of Crotona Park in the Bronx. He then led a sit-in at Borough President James Lyons' office, demanding use of athletic equipment not being used by whites. The sit-in succeeded.

In 1960, Dr. Matthew joined the first contingent to picket the American Medical Association in Atlantic City. He still refuses to join the National AMA because it allows segregation to exist in some of the local chapters.

When he was head of Interfaith Hospital, Dr. Matthew became aware of the economic force that he was wielding. A 160-bed hospital hires, trains, and maintains a sizable work force; it also buys huge quantities of products and services. Dr. Matthew conceived the idea of building a complex of business enterprises using the hospital as the cornerstone. Each of the enterprises could be used to help Negroes help themselves. He would hire untrained Negroes most of whom were on welfare, teach them a skill or trade, and get them started into the mainstream of American life.

At the apex of his organization is NEGRO, a nonprofit holding company financed through the sale of bonds in denominations as small as twenty-five cents. The organization now has assets of $3.5 million. In addition to the hospital, there is a chemical company, a clothing company, a construction company, a retail store, three bus lines, and half a dozen service projects.

The chemical company, which is a natural outgrowth of the hospital laboratory, is working three shifts producing a food

disinfectant to prevent amoebic dysentery in Vietnam and
regions of the U. S. South, a developer for wire photos, and
fire extinguisher charges. Its latest venture is into the manu-
facture of paint. Dr. Matthew reasons that the hospital and
construction company, both of which use quantities of paint,
will provide a base for the profitable sale of this product.

Most of the employees of the chemical company are drug
addicts. Dr. Matthew says that he has the most successful
program for drug-addiction rehabilitation in the country. He
guarantees any drug addict a job, the chance to learn a skill
or trade, and a decent place to live. In return, they must put
themselves under the hospital's medical care. The doctor con-
tends that most Negroes are not forced into addiction because
of personality problems, as is the case with most white addicts;
Negroes become addicted because of their inability to function
in society simply because of the color of their skin. By guar-
anteeing them a place in the scheme of things, NEGRO meets
the basic needs of the colored addicts.

The clothing company has a lingerie factory, two dress
factories, a coat factory, and a boutique which is a retail out-
let. It too got its start because of the hospital and still makes
the hospital's sheets and bed clothing.

The construction company is involved in new construction
and rehabilitation. It has rehabilitated about five hundred
housing units in New York ghettos. Hundreds are awaiting
rehabilitation, but the company must move slowly because it
lacks the money to expand rapidly.

These rehabilitated units house mostly mothers with children
who have no men to care for them. Dr. Matthew guarantees
anyone entering these buildings a job, and he trains them in a
skill. He sets up nurseries to care for the children while the
mothers are working. He has a cleaning service that keeps
the units in good condition. He even has a dietary service. By

central purchasing, he can buy food cheaper and ensure a balanced diet. Menus are planned three months in advance, and the families can elect to cook in their own rooms or eat in a central dining room.

The change in the lives of most of these people is radical. Many had never before experienced a sense of urgency. They never heard an alarm clock go off meaning that they had to get up, dress, and go somewhere. This complete unfamiliarity with discipline constitutes the prime reason for society's considering them hard-core unemployables.

Dr. Matthew is now opening preschool schools in order to change the lives of the children. Besides giving them a chance to experience discipline, he also gives them an opportunity to learn some basic social amenities. For example, they can see what a table looks like when it is set for a meal. For before Dr. Matthew entered their lives, many of them never sat for a family meal; they were accustomed to spooning food from a pot on the stove.

NEGRO operates three bus lines: one in the ghetto of Watts in Los Angeles, one in the ghetto of South Jamaica in Queens, and one in the ghetto of Harlem in Manhattan. The one in Watts is operating successfully; the two in New York are operating without a city franchise.

The whole problem started in Jamaica where for twenty years the Negro community has asked for bus service, and politicians have promised but never delivered. The bus service in the area was so poor that many of the people had to walk twenty blocks and take three buses, at a cost of twenty cents each, to get to work. Dr. Matthew found this out because it was happening to several employees at Interfaith Hospital.

In the summer of 1967, discontent over the bus service, among other things, placed South Jamaica, a community of 100,000 people, on the thin edge of a riot. And since the ghetto is within half a block of the seventh largest shopping center in the United States, a riot there would have made all the others that took place pale by comparison. Dr. Matthew stepped in and put two buses in the area. And even though his line was not franchised, the city was grateful and let the buses run.

In December, the city decided to shut down the bus line, and it got a court order to that effect. Dr. Matthew promptly opened another bus line in Harlem, but he stopped charging fares. However, he does not discourage his passengers from purchasing twenty-five cent bonds when they ride the buses. "I am not in favor of lawlessness. I am testing this particular law because it is not meant to set standards but to keep people out. If I break the law, I should go to jail. We're seeking reform, not 'revolution.'"

The city, of course, is embarrassed by the whole affair. Everyone knows that the bus service in the ghettos had been hopelessly inadequate before Dr. Matthew stepped in. And if the city jails him for trying to help Negroes help themselves, the adverse publicity will be devastating.

Meanwhile, Dr. Matthew sends ten unfranchised buses on gypsylike trips through Harlem and Queens, picking up passengers where it finds them and taking them where they want to go. He appears on radio and television across the nation, explaining his position in the case. Many newspaper stories have appeared about the impasse. And what is the city doing? When asked, the franchise commissioner admitted that a report had come in that the buses were operating. A reporter asked what action the city intended to take. "First," said the commissioner, "we have to decide whether it was an isolated incident." As yet, the city has not decided.

At this point, NEGRO can be adjudged a financial success

but on a small scale. People are buying the bonds, and the earnings from the various enterprises are more than enough to meet the interest payments and redeem the bonds. But so far, no major investor has stepped in. Dr. Matthew has urged the government to establish a program similar to the Marshall Plan to invest money in Negroes who want to help themselves. He would like government help, but not as a handout. The government, however, is geared only to give money through its various welfare projects.

Dr. Matthew has even written a widely publicized open letter to President Johnson, telling him why the war on poverty does not meet the needs of the Negro people and seeking loans for a program that does meet the Negro needs. He pointed out that even David Rockefeller has said that NEGRO's program "is the most imaginative, productive, hopeful, and genuine self-help program in existence."

In his letter to the President, Dr. Matthew did say something which stirred up some dust. He said that if our government wouldn't help, he would seek loans from foreign nations:

> We feel that we should inform you, Mr. President, of this decision. It is not our intent to do anything not in the best interest of our country. We want to be certain that there are no regulations prohibiting a private non-profit organization of citizens soliciting aid from foreign nations. If such negotiations require clearance from the State Department, we will be happy to comply.

Although he made no formal requests for foreign loans, the word was out, and offers as well as inquiries started pouring in. Naturally, the Soviet Union proved the most anxious of all to loan money. However, this occurred at a time when U. S. prestige abroad was at a particularly low ebb. Dr. Matthew was urged by many groups not to embarrass the government, so he refused to accept any offers of help from foreign nations. And there the matter rests.

The charters of most funds and foundations prohibit them also from investing money in self-help projects. They are geared only for charities. So Dr. Matthew is still forced to move ahead slowly with his projects.

But his ultimate plans are staggering in concept. He sees NEGRO rehabilitating and changing the lives of his race in all the ghettos across the nation. "Negroes are still in a primitive economic state. We will have to develop a kind of group orientation to work with one another, to teach one another skills, to find one another jobs, to change our standard of living, and to change our behavior. Only then will we be ready to integrate and make it work."

And where will all the money for this grandiose scheme come from? "You don't have to be black to buy NEGRO bonds," says Dr. Matthew.

Meshulam Riklis

Ever since an enterprising Stone Age man used a branch from a fallen tree to move a boulder from the entrance to his cave, people have been capitalizing on the principle of leverage. Archimedes became so enthused with the power of leverage that he said he could move the whole world if he could find a place to stand.

Meshulam Riklis started using financial leverage fourteen years ago. So far he has not moved the world. But he has obtained control of companies doing over a billion and a half dollars of business with assets of over half a billion dollars and about 100,000 employees, and the end is not in sight. His empire includes control over companies manufacturing men's and women's apparel, chemicals, various building materials, and stores selling just about everything else.

Someone recently asked him how he would describe himself, and he answered: "As a rapid American." This was an apt answer because the Rapid American Corporation represents the base from which he controls his family of companies.

Meshulam's rise to his present position as head of this far-flung empire has not been accomplished without his having to overcome Herculean problems. He had to have the courage to stick with his ideas about leverage when it seemed as if the whole financial community had turned its back on him. He has been maligned, accused, threatened, and sued for daring to be different. And through it all, perhaps because of it all, he has emerged as one of the great powers on the business scene.

To the average businessman, the principle of financial leverage refers simply to situations where businesses are better off raising money through borrowing rather than selling stock. The rule of thumb is to borrow if the cost of the money is less than the business will earn from its use.

To Meshulam Riklis, leverage is a way to build an empire that can grow at a geometric rate with virtually no personal cash investment except at the beginning of a series of acquisitions. In a fascinating thesis, which he wrote to earn his master's degree in business administration from Ohio State University, he explains how he did this and arrived where he was a few years ago. Now, he has moved considerably farther but still within the framework of his original master plan.

The magic formula that he has followed occurred to him fourteen years earlier, when he was in his second year of postgraduate work at Ohio State. One of his professors had assigned him the task of trying to find a company with more cash behind each share of stock than the market price of the stock.

To Meshulam, this semed like a fool's errand. He couldn't imagine a going concern underpriced to the extent that the cash assets alone, not counting the value of its other current and fixed assets, would exceed the total market value of the stock. And yet, he found that such companies exist. In the process, he became so excited with the leverage implication that he did not quite complete his master's degree and began to seek his fortune in the business world.

Meshulam knew that he needed two things before he could start accumulating companies through his newborn ideas on leverage. He needed more intimate knowledge of the complex world of finance, and seed money with which to make his first major purchase. Accordingly, he took a job as a security analyst with Piper, Jaffray and Hopwood, a brokerage firm in Minneapolis.

To supplement his income, he also took a part-time job teaching Hebrew to children in the area. Because of his present reputation in the intricate world of Wall Street finance, few people realize that Meshulam immigrated to this country only twenty-one years ago. He came from Israel where he received most of his early education. In fact, he still transacts confidential business matters in such busy places as Wall Street or a barbershop by speaking in Hebrew.

As an analyst, Meshulam soon developed a sophisticated knowledge of stocks, bonds, options, warrants, and convertibles. He also gained more insight into the phenomenon of cash-rich and underpriced companies. Probably most important, he learned how psychological factors affect stock prices. Today, he is so astute in these matters that he not only welcomes the give and take of a security analysts' luncheon but he even takes advantage of the occasions to lecture the analysts on some of the more esoteric forms of financial pyrotechnics.

Meshulam soon learned that, in addition to other considerations, a low market price of a stock can reflect investor disgust with an entrenched management that refuses to alter its outmoded ways of doing business. Thus, although fundamental considerations such as asset values and earnings should influence the price, these can be negated by the backwardness of management. Oddly, an almost sure sign of an ultraconservative management is an overabundance of cash in the bank. The productivity level of the company's return on its capital suffers from too much inactive cash. So does the company's growth.

After he felt that he had sufficient practical knowledge about finance, he took the next step toward his goal of using leverage to build a financial empire. He became a stockbroker, or what's known in the industry as a customer's man.

He took this new job because he realized that he not only had to make more money so he would have some to use as down payment on his master plan, but he also had to raise considerably more than he alone could put together. As a customer's man, he knew that he would meet the influential investors who, if he were persuasive, could form the nucleus of an investment syndicate.

In 1953, with half a million dollars he raised through his first syndicate, he made his first move. He bought controlling interest in Gruen Watch Company. But this attempt failed. Although his investment in Gruen resulted in his realizing a substantial profit, his lack of practical operating experience led him to appoint another man as president of the company. Soon, he found himself in conflict over the direction that the company should take. When it came to a showdown, some of the members of his syndicate backed the president instead of Meshulam. Meshulam sold his stock (at a good profit) and started looking again for a company which he could use as his initial lever.

With $25,000 of his own money and an additional $350,000 put together by a syndicate, he bought controlling interest in Rapid Electrotype, a company that was to prove to be a perfect home base for his expansion plans.

What first attracted him to Rapid was its $2.3 million cash assets and only $600,000 liabilities. The stock was selling for $17 and, with only 124,000 shares outstanding, all but one dollar of the per share market price was backed by cash.

Rapid Electrotype was controlled by the officers who worked for it and by a seventy-year-old chairman of the board who owned 10 percent of the stock. This simplified Meshulam's problem of approaching the owners with an offer to buy. From

the point of view of the stockholders, Meshulam's offer to buy
stock for $11 a share over the market price was exceptionally
attractive for this lusterless company. However, it was also a
good price from Meshulam's point of view, because he was
convinced that the company which was earning over $200,000
a year after taxes was underpriced by at least $16 a share.

As soon as he gained control of Rapid Electrotype, Meshulam made his next move. Using Rapid's assets to raise money,
he purchased 40 percent of the stock of Smith-Corona (now
SCM). This was enough to give him two seats on Smith-
Corona's board of directors. Meshulam then tried to get Smith-
Corona to buy Kleinschmidt Laboratories, but the board was
reluctant to expand through debt financing. Instead, its members decided to buy Kleinschmidt Laboratories with common
stock. This, as the board was perfectly aware, had the effect of
shrinking Meshulam's 40 percent ownership. Meshulam saw
that he and the board were at loggerheads, and he sold his
Smith-Corona holdings for $320,000 profit.

His next purchase through Rapid Electrotype was 51 percent of American Colortype. After selling off some of the
liquid properties, Meshulam was now engaged in electrotypes,
mats, mail order, paint manufacturing, plastic-packaging
manufacturing, citrus groves, metal-sign manufacturing, and
children's wear. But his interest was not in the kind of business that he was in; it was in the possibilities of generating
leverage money through a merger of Rapid Electrotype and
American Colortype.

Within six months, American Colortype had $6 million
cash in the banks. Rapid Electrotype, which owed only $1
million to the banks, had 51 percent control over this money.
As a result, Meshulam was in a strategic position to make
some new power moves. He bought control of Butler Brothers,
a midwest chain store operation. In three years under his

control the company prospered while he increased the ownership to 51 percent. At the same time, he consolidated his Rapid
Electrotype with the now almost liquidated American Colortype. Consistent with his method of planning ahead and following a direct path leading to his goal, he eventually sold
the assets of Butler Brothers to City Products Corp. This sale
gave him a $15 million profit and $50 million cash which was
the springboard to his largest and most important acquisition
program.

Two weeks after the sale of Butler Brothers, he used the
money to buy enough shares to control United Stores and to
acquire 10 percent of H. L. Green. Jointly, these variety companies in turn gave him control of McCrory-McLellan variety
stores. This purchase marked the beginning of his troubles as
well as the cornerstone of his eventual success.

He then bought Oklahoma Tire and Supply Company for a
combination of cash and subordinated notes. He bought National Shirt Shops through cash and a stock swap of preferred
stock for common. He increased his ownership of H. L. Green
to over 50 percent through cash purchases of that company's
stock. He bought Economy Auto Stores for cash. He acquired
Lerner Shops through a combination of cash, subordinated
debentures, and warrants.

His purchase of Lerner Shops serves as a classic example of
sophisticated financial leverage. At the time, Lerner's common
stock was selling for $23, with 1.25 million shares outstanding.
Meshulam was fairly confident that he could acquire enough
to get control of the company if he offered $40 a share. How-
ever, he did not want to dissipate McCrory's available cash,
and he felt that the McCrory's common and convertible preferred stock was more valuable than its market price at that
time. He also felt that short-term debt was out of the question

because he had just taken on an $18 million short-term debt to buy Oklahoma Tire and Supply.

This left him with one attractive alternative: a long-term debenture with small payouts for a number of years, increasing with time and ballooning at the end of fifteen years. However, he realized that such a note would sell at a discount of 10 to 15 percent of its face value. He says, "An additional sweetener was required here to balance the difference between the market value of the debenture and its face value, but it had to be created as a marketable commodity without penalizing the issuer. Warrants were utilized for this purpose."

What Meshulam finally did was offer a combination of one debenture with a face value of $40 plus one and a half warrants to buy McCrory stock at $20 a share (the stock at the time was selling for $16 a share). The debenture at a 15 percent discount was worth about $34, and the warrant was worth about $9. When the offer became known, the price of McCrory stock started moving up, making the warrant worth more. The offer became so attractive that Meshulam was able to acquire more than 90 percent of the total stock outstanding.

By 1962, Meshulam Riklis was chairman of the board and president of Rapid-American Corporation which in turn owned 51 percent of McCrory Corporation. McCrory Corporation controlled Oklahoma Tire and Supply, National Shirt Shops, Lerner Shops, H. L. Green, and Economy Stores. Meshulam had built his empire and was widely acclaimed as a financial wizard. It was at this high point in his career that things started to go wrong.

Just as leverage can explain how Meshulam was able to acquire so much in so little time, leverage also was at the root of his troubles—for when you build on borrowed money, you've got to have sufficient earnings to meet fixed interest charges and a schedule of repayments. In 1962, everything seemed to go wrong with Meshulam's empire.

Rapid-American suffered unexpected capital losses amounting to $9.3 million. Four and a half million of this came from the write-off of notes due Rapid for the sale of American Paper Specialty Company, a company that had been spun off from the old American Colortype Company. Meshulam had sold this company to its management for a price that was twenty times after earnings. However, as soon as the new owner took over, the company started to go downhill.

In addition, Rapid's mail order division had to be written off in that year. This operation had never been very successful, and its 1962 losses were tremendous. The liquidation resulted in a capital loss of $4.7 million.

These losses, in a company that couldn't be expected to earn more than half a million dollars in a good year, were huge. Meshulam began to realize that he was in serious trouble unless McCrory made a substantial profit to offset Rapid's dismal financial performance.

But McCrory was not living up to expectations. At the start of the year, Meshulam predicted an after-tax profit for the company of $10 million. The first eight months showed a loss of $2.3 million compared with an expected profit of $373,000. Of course, the last quarter is always the best in a retail-oriented corporation, but McCrory would have needed a sensational final quarter to live up to Meshulam's predictions.

In October, *Barrons* published a highly critical article about Meshulam's operations. The price of McCrory stock began to fall and so did that of Rapid-American. This created the need for Rapid to put up more collateral for some of its loans, but the company had already exhausted its resources.

At the end of the year, McCrory earned only $3.8 million after taxes. The banks increased their pressure on Meshulam, and he had no alternative except to start liquidating holdings to raise cash. He started stripping Rapid-American of all holdings except McCrory. He tried to sell Lerner Shops to Glen Alden Corporation but was blocked by the stockholders.

In 1963, he sold thirty Yellow Front supermarkets, grocery stores, and a warehouse for $1 million. He sold a paint division for $2.5 million. In January, 1964, he sold National Shirt Shops for $5 million.

Realizing also that most of his companies' problems stemmed from poor operating controls in the variety division, he devoted himself to improving operations. He set up better controls and developed better management personnel in the daily operating duties. His efforts turned the company around. By the end of 1964, McCrory realized a net income of $8.67 million. In 1965, its net income jumped to $10.06 million; in 1966, it increased to $10.57 million.

By October, 1964, Meshulam was once again applying leverage to expand his McCrory holdings. He bought control of Glen Alden. In 1966, he acquired control of S. Klein department stores for a package of debentures and warrants. In October of that year, he acquired the assets of sixteen Best & Company stores located in Massachusetts, Connecticut, New York, New Jersey, Pennsylvania, Maryland, Virginia, and the District of Columbia. He financed four fifths of the cash price with a short-term note.

In August, 1967, he announced a directors' agreement to merge S. Klein into McCrory. In June, Lerner Shops announced a tender offer to acquire all common shares not already held by McCrory in exchange for cash, debentures, and warrants. In December, Glen Alden, which is 44 percent owned by McCrory, merged with Stanley Warner Corporation. This was after Glen Alden had acquired control of and merged with two giants—Philip Carey ($100 million sales in the building material field) and the BVD Company.

Meanwhile, Rapid-American Corporation, aside from its McCrory leverage situation, went on an acquisition trail of its own. In December, 1965, it purchased 100 percent of Joseph H. Cohen & Sons, one of the largest manufacturers of tailored men's apparel. In 1967, it acquired 100 percent of Leeds Travelwear, Inc., a luggage and sporting goods manufacturer. Meshulam says that he expects to bring about a maximum utilization of these two companies to increase by acquisition. Put simply, this means that he intends to use these companies as levers for Rapid-American just as he has done with McCrory.

The chart on page 67 represents Meshulam's progress in using leverage to date. If he can continue on this acquisition route for another fourteen years, he should be in control of something in excess of ten times his present empire, for his growth, like that of populations, is in a geometric rather than arithmetic ratio. In finance at least, he may have found the position that Archimedes was looking for. Before he is through, he may yet move the world.

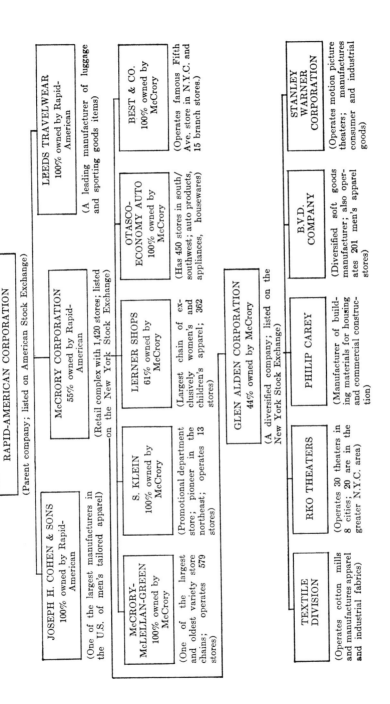

RAPID-AMERICAN CORPORATION
(Parent company; listed on American Stock Exchange)

JOSEPH H. COHEN & SONS
100% owned by Rapid-American
(One of the largest manufacturers in the U.S. of men's tailored apparel)

McCRORY CORPORATION
55% owned by Rapid-American
(Retail complex with 1,420 stores; listed on the New York Stock Exchange)

LEEDS TRAVELWEAR
100% owned by Rapid-American
(A leading manufacturer of luggage and sporting goods items)

McCRORY-McLELLAN-GREEN
100% owned by McCrory
(One of the largest and oldest variety store chains; operates 579 stores)

S. KLEIN
100% owned by McCrory
(Promotional department store; pioneer in the northeast; operates 13 stores)

LERNER SHOPS
61% owned by McCrory
(Largest chain of exclusively women's and children's apparel; 362 stores)

OTASCO-ECONOMY AUTO
100% owned by McCrory
(Has 450 stores in south/southwest; auto products, appliances, housewares)

BEST & CO.
100% owned by McCrory
(Operates famous Fifth Ave. store in N.Y.C. and 15 branch stores.)

GLEN ALDEN CORPORATION
44% owned by McCrory
(A diversified company; listed on the New York Stock Exchange)

TEXTILE DIVISION
(Operates cotton mills and manufactures apparel and industrial fabrics)

RKO THEATERS
(Operates 30 theaters in 8 cities; 20 are in the greater N.Y.C. area)

PHILIP CAREY
(Manufacturer of building materials for housing and commercial construction)

B.V.D. COMPANY
(Diversified soft goods manufacturer; also operates 201 men's apparel stores)

STANLEY WARNER CORPORATION
(Operates motion picture theaters; manufactures consumer and industrial goods)

Virginia Graham

Virginia Graham dares to be different by being completely herself. She meets life's unexpected vagaries with unpremeditated candor. She has no inhibitions that dilute her fantastically warm and pervasive personality. She also has a penchant for "happenings." Virginia attributes this to the fact that she's a non-conformist living in a world that's mostly peopled with conformists. "I believe that things happen to people who are not conformists. A conformist doesn't look at the right or left—he's too busy walking straight ahead. Most people are so deep in self-preoccupation that they don't really see what's going on on all sides of them. My brother and I, however, saw everything on all sides of us and got into everything."

Happenings started for her when she was very young. Once, she experimented with a new fountain pen by writing her name and address on a menu in a Chinese restaurant. A few days later, the first of a series of threatening letters arrived. For a time, the family ignored the letters but, when the threats became more vicious, Virginia's father turned the letters over to the police. The police decided to use Virginia as a decoy. As instructed in one of the letters, she walked one Sunday morning to Chicago's Lincoln Monument. "I went to the appointed place without money and with policemen behind every tree, guns drawn. They apprehended a pathetic, mentally ill fellow who recognized the name Komiss from my father's department store and thought he could get something for nothing. That's the kind of thing I put my parents through."

She was a near-witness to the St. Valentine's Day massacre. The killings took place in a garage within half a block from where she was standing with friends outside the Francis W. Parker school in Chicago. She even watched the getaway car roar by and then went to peek into the garage. "While the other kids screamed and fainted, I ran to the phone to notify the *Chicago Tribune*. Mine was one of the first reports of gangland's celebrated massacre."

Once when she was still in her early teens, she had an invitation to be a gangster's moll. At the time, she and her father were staying at the Arlington Hotel in Hot Springs, Arkansas. A man walked up to her, told her his name was Luciano and said, "I've been watching you. You're my type. You come back to New York, and I'll show you the time of your life—mink coat and everything."

"Is that the way they treat visitors in New York?" Virginia asked innocently.

That night, the hotel doctor diagnosed a bronchial infection she had as whooping cough. Virginia was isolated in a cottage and did not emerge until "Lucky" Luciano, the notorious gangster who was involved in narcotics traffic and white slavery, had departed.

Although she has only one brother, Virginia's childhood was actually spent in a large-family environment. Both her father and her mother came from families of eleven children. Once a month, the relatives converged for a family picnic. "It was such fun—such laughter, such carefree times. I used to see Papa almost as if an eraser had passed over his face, all the troubled lines of responsibility and worry wiped off as if by magic."

Mr. Komiss owned a department store in downtown Chicago, and almost all his employees were relatives. "This was Papa's idea. He always used to say that there would be no need for organized charity if every family took care of its own."

With most people, it's easy to separate their personal lives from their careers. With Virginia, it's impossible. Her father and mother, her husband, her daughter, her volunteer charities, and her professional career are so tightly interwoven that it's hard to tell where one leaves off and another begins. Her family, for example, exerted a profound influence on her. Her attachment to her parents has never abated. To her, her father who has been dead for many years remains a living presence and constant mentor. "His love for me was a blanket of warmth, the comfort of which I will feel, I think, forever. 'Who turned on the lights? Who let in the sunshine?' he would ask when I came in the room." And her mother, who taught Virginia discipline, also exerted a lasting influence: "Now that I am older, I realize how much I owe my mother. She helped me by creating a terrible frustration in me—a frustration to make myself into somebody, to be someone, to win from her somehow a word of praise or affection."

Actually, Virginia probably inherited her uninhibited responses to life's stimuli from her mother. For her mother is as much a nonconformist as Virginia. When, for example, Ralph Edwards tried to contact Mrs. Komiss to arrange for Virginia's appearance on *This Is Your Life,* she wouldn't believe that he was actually Ralph Edwards. She thought that Ralph was her son, Juddy, playing a practical joke. She hung up on him repeatedly. Later, Ralph phoned at the family department store and traced Mrs. Komiss to the coat department. Juddy happened to be with her. Suddenly, she realized she was talking to the real Ralph Edwards. She fainted.

In many respects, Virginia's childhood was quite ordinary for a child born to a well-to-do family. At fifteen, she and the family made the grand tour of the United States and Canada. When she graduated from high school, she attended the National Park Seminary, an expensive finishing school in Forest Glen, Maryland. There, she learned how to walk properly, shake hands, remember names, type, and take shorthand. She also became a blonde, thanks to seven hours spent in a beauty parlor called Pierre's. When the dean of the school saw the hair, he restricted Virginia to campus for two months. But the minute she got out, she returned to Pierre's to get the roots touched up. When her mother saw the hair, she bought a bottle of black dye and applied it. Virginia in turn got a bottle of peroxide and used it. "This went on three times in two weeks—blonde to black, black to blonde, blonde to black. My father finally said, 'One of you is going to have to give in or she'll be bald.' That was how I became a blonde."

She finished her schooling at the University of Chicago and Northwestern. Her first job was door-to-door selling. The product, fittingly enough in view of her future interest in cosmetics and beauty aids, was a formula-type cosmetic to take dirt off women's faces.

In the fall of 1935, Virginia made a trip to Long Island to visit her former roommate from National Park Seminary. While there, she went to a costume party with a blind date named Harry Guttenberg. "He was dressed as a barnyard character. To what I later learned was a very handsome Roman nose, he had added a wad of putty. In my sweet, clear voice that was like an air-raid alert, I sang out, 'I know the costume's a fake, but don't tell me the face is real!'"

At the end of two weeks, Harry Guttenberg proposed marriage. Since the two were perfectly suited for one another, it was a marriage that was and still is ideal. Even from a financial point of view, Harry was a good catch because he was head of Louis Guttenberg and Sons, the most famous costume house in the East.

Virginia had had a serious operation when she was nineteen. As a result, she and Harry resigned themselves to a childless marriage. But nine months and four days after the marriage, Virginia gave birth to a daughter. Lynn is now a beautiful woman, but she apparently got off to an inauspicious start! "People would walk up to the carriage and say, 'Oh, let's see the baby,' with anticipatory elation lighting their faces, and then at the first sight of the child—complete silence, a step back, and, 'What a personality!' or 'What lovely ears, so nice and close to her head.' Hoping to spare her from this unflattering scrutiny, I put Lynn on her face for six months, explaining that it was good for the shape of her head. It was my mother-in-law, God rest her soul, who was the only one who said, 'She'll grow up to be the most beautiful girl.' I only hope that wherever she is, she knows how right she was!"

Oddly, Virginia Graham's working career started in earnest shortly after Lynn's birth. Since she had a nurse for the baby and a maid for the apartment, Virginia had time on her hands. She applied for a job with WMCA radio station in New York. The station's manager told her she could have a job if she could come up with some improved ideas for the commercials aired over *Grandstand and Bandstand,* a three-hour-a-day program featuring sports, music, and advice to the lovelorn. Virginia conceived the idea, which is now a common practice, of having the sports and music celebrities appearing on the program sponsor the products.

Not long after she got the job, she started ghost-writing for the famous actress Mae Murray who was doing the advice to the lovelorn on the program. Later, she took over a cooking show on the station. "Soon they called me the Ulcer Queen because I killed off more people that year than the virus."

When Lynn was two and a half years old, Harry and Virginia decided to move to the suburbs. They bought a house in Great Neck, Long Island, and Virginia set out to acquaint herself with her new environs. "I drove around a great deal to get to know the area. I always have to know exactly where everything is and what's going on. One of the first things I discovered was that the Red Cross was organizing a new motor corps. What better way to meet people in my community and become involved with other women who would be civic minded and aware?"

The purpose of the motor corps was to replace male ambulance drivers who were going to war. Virginia joined just before World War II started and stayed until 1947. She became involved in "everything the Red Cross had to offer— Gray Ladies, nurses' aides, first-aid instruction, motor corps."

In 1947, she attended a meeting of fourteen women to discuss cerebral palsy. This marked the beginning of her volunteer work for charities. "I wonder if the world will ever know how much of the entire success of United Cerebral Palsy, and every other charity I have worked on, can be attributed to the volunteers? Without volunteer women, causes in the communities would die. Women are the heart, the pulse, and the reason for the development of the sense of obligation."

She became one of the first entertainers who traveled around to volunteer groups, raising money for the causes. Usually, she would act as commentator at fashion shows. Her approach was to make the event memorable by teasing the models and the fashions. She was just starting to realize her ability to captivate audiences by the sheer power of her personality.

One day, she decided to adopt the stage name of Virginia

Graham because a fortune-teller predicted that she was on the threshold of an important career as an entertainer. The fortune-teller was the one who suggested the name Graham. In time, Virginia was to discover that Graham is such a nondescript name that people have difficulty remembering it. This is the reason for the title of her deeply moving autobiography, *There Goes What's Her Name.*

Virginia's fashion commentaries for charities led to some professional jobs. She was invited to address the beauticians at one of New York's International Beauty Shows. Her outspoken criticism of beauticians who do not use the products and services they sell was so hilarious and well-received that she was invited to return for four years running. One of those years, she appeared as a representative of the show on Dave Garroway's television program *Today.* This in turn led to her taking over Dave Garroway's spot for a week while he was vacationing.

Another time, United Cerebral Palsy arranged for her to do the commentary for a fashion show for hats on the *Ed Herlihy TV Show.* This earned her an invitation to audition as replacement for a girl doing an unsponsored cooking show on NBC-TV. Virginia missed getting that job by a day because the girl she was to replace found a sponsor at the last minute.

Her next opportunity came when she was invited to be a guest on a television program called *Zeke Manners and His Beverly Hillbillies.* After her appearance, Zeke received so many phone calls urging him to bring Virginia back that he offered her a full-time job for $100 a week. At the time, Virginia had two agents. "We split the $100 three ways, and for $35 a week, or $7 a day, I cheerfully became a star on a two-hour daily TV show. And you thought TV automatically brought big money!"

She finally lost this job when Zeke was asked by AFTRA

to pay Virginia union scale. This would have meant $800 a week. Instead Zeke fired her.

In 1951, Virginia found that she had cancer. For the next five years, her happiness was to be marred by the twin specters of death and tragedy hovering over her. At first, she couldn't cope with the news because she was sure the doctor was pronouncing her death sentence. She was told only two hours after she had undergone surgery in the hospital. She remembered how her father always told her that God's ways are not to be questioned.

Harry fared even worse. His mind began withdrawing almost as soon as he was told of Virginia's condition. Within months he was in the depths of a violent nervous breakdown. He had to undergo numerous shock treatments. And to add to his troubles, his family business burned down at a time when he had almost no insurance coverage.

His condition was so serious that Virginia was forced to forget her own troubles to care for him. Indeed, her resiliency was such that she snapped back into a good mental attitude right after she underwent major surgery for her condition. "If anyone lost weight, it was the X-ray technicians. The very first time I appeared for treatment, they stripped me, put me on a table, and began marking off my stomach with a big blue pencil. I said, 'You know, from the air I must look subdivided just like Levittown. Tell me, do you think the waterfront property is more valuable?' "

When the costume business burned, Harry was too sick to help revive the company. It was Virginia who found another building, rented it, hired seamstresses, and began the laborious and costly task of creating a new inventory of costumes for the firm. She kept the firm alive until he recovered sufficiently to take charge once again. In time, both Harry and the business recovered completely.

In 1952, Virginia was invited to try out for a television show called *Food for Thought*. She got this opportunity because the wife of the producer was an old fan of hers from when Virginia was appearing on the Zeke Manners show. *"Virginia Graham and Food for Thought* stayed on the air from 1952 until 1957, a spirited venture in communications run by an inexperienced technician and an amateur star without a single motion picture or Broadway credit. Where did she come from? A by-product of TV who cast her bread on the water by doing work for charity, invited on the Zeke Manners show, seen by a woman viewer whose husband put her on his show. Through the friendship of women, through the devotion and loyalty of women, I have gotten where I am today."

She made scores of appearances for benefits. She had an uncanny knack of being able to reach responsive chords in the hearts of her listeners. On one famous occasion, during a telethon for arthritis in New York, she started a veritable avalanche of money pouring in by telling the audience about her ordeal with cancer. "Once I had begun, I couldn't stop. I had to go on talking about the fright, the fear, the anxiety, the prayers to God, the pleading to live. I had to tell it all. The music was playing in the background. Someone thought of 'You'll Never Walk Alone.' When I stopped, I broke down and wept. Up to that minute I had never shed a tear. Not a single tear over my illness, or Harry's illness, or all the things we had been through. I wept and the audience wept."

Her numerous appearances on telethons endeared her to thousands of people whom she had never seen in person. Letters started pouring in to Ralph Edwards to put Virginia on *This Is Your Life*. Finally, he did. And this appearance, in turn, led to her getting a job teamed with Mike Wallace on *Weekday*, an NBC network radio shop. "For a frantic six months, I was doing both *Food for Thought* on local TV and *Weekday*

on network radio every day. I had an unbelievable schedule. I
worked from ten until four on *Weekday*. I would get off the
air at ten of four and let Mike do the closing minutes. I had
a taxi waiting for me. I'd leave Radio City at ten of four and
at four o'clock I'd be at Dumont on East 67th Street where
at four thirty I went on television for half an hour."

All this was prologue from the point of view of Virginia's
career. Her big break and her step into the national limelight
came with a series of appearances on the Jack Paar show. Her
first appearance was dominated by another performer, but
Jack Paar, who was bombarded by phone calls and letters from
Virginia's friends, gave her a second chance. "That was the
night I said, 'Jack, you don't know the mail I got after my
first time here. I had a letter from a fellow who went to school
with me. I hadn't seen him since I was eight years old. My
maiden name was Komiss. And Whitney wrote, "You are
Ginny Komiss, aren't you? I'm sure of it. Because who else
can look like two June Allysons?" ' "

For their twenty-fifth wedding anniversary, Virginia and
Harry gave themselves a European trip as a present. When
they returned, Virginia took an ambassadorial job for Clairol.
For seven years, she traveled around the country, appearing
on platforms with models, top fashion designers, and leading
store executives. Since Harry had built enough depth in management in his business to leave it for extended periods, he
accompanied her wherever she went. "All hotel reservations
were to be made in the name of Mr. and Mrs. Harry Guttenberg. Letters would inform the people who were to meet us
what my married name was and instruct them to address
Harry as Mr. Guttenberg."

In 1962, Virginia launched a television program that has
proved to be a perfect vehicle for her particular brand of conversational pyrotechnics. It is ABC television's *Girl Talk*,

directed by Monty Morgan. Virginia attributes a great part
of the success of *Girl Talk* to Monty Morgan's ability to select
guests who will generate sparks when they are brought together for unrehearsed conversations. "He has an infallible
sense of the wrong people who will be right together." But
what makes the whole thing work week after week and situation after situation is the excitement brought to the program
by the presence of Virginia Graham. Her guests may detest
one another, but they have Virginia as a common denominator;
they love her and regard her as their friend. "I have spoken
eye level from the time I was born. I talk eye level to everybody. That's my real secret weapon."

It's hard for someone who has not been behind the scenes to
appreciate the problems of putting together a show like *Girl
Talk*. When the guests arrive at the studio, most of them are
nervous enough to jump out of their skins. Even though the
outcome of the program is more important to Virginia than
the guest, she must turn on her warmth to soothe the guest and
assure her that she's lovely and is going to be marvelous on
the program. To add to the problem, the guest is usually dis-
concerted when she discovers who else will be appearing on the
program. Often Virginia has to separate her guests like opposing camps and to travel back and forth between them like
a labor mediator. Since she tapes as many as three consecutive
shows in a single session, her job sometimes takes on the
aspects of an extended nightmare. And yet, she somehow retains her sanity, her sense of humor, and her steadfast conviction that everyone she meets deserves understanding and
affection.

To Virginia, *Girl Talk* does not mark the end of her career.
It's the beginning. She has made her stage debut in the starring
role of *Late Love* at the Pheasant Run Playhouse near Chicago, and starred in 1967 in *Barefoot in the Park*. She and

Jean Libman Block have written a new Meredith Press book about beauty care called *Don't Blame the Mirror*. This year, she has launched a new line of clothes, Thayer Knits for Virginia Graham. She has a cookbook coming out soon. Her autobiography *There Goes What's Her Name* has sold nearly a million copies.

"When people bemoan the difficult times in which we are living and challenge my excitement and joy in life, I have to tell them that forgetting has been my necessity and looking forward my salvation. I look forward to the future because, in words I once heard and have never forgotten, the future is where I expect to spend the rest of my life."

Maxwell Maltz, M.D.

Dr. Maxwell Maltz has spent his lifetime changing the images of others. He started with external images at a time when it took great courage to enter the field of plastic surgery. Later, when he switched to changing internal images, he dared to lay a hard-won international reputation as a physician on the line to promulgate a new psychological theory.

When Dr. Maltz chose the field of plastic surgery after graduating from the College of Physicians and Surgeons at Columbia, there weren't more than half a dozen men practicing that specialty in this country. He had to go to Europe for his postgraduate work. In England, he studied under Harold D. Gillies, the famous English surgeon who in World War I was in charge of the plastic surgery division of the British Army. In Germany, he studied under Jacques Joseph who perfected the technique of correcting nasal disfigurements without leaving a scar. He also studied under the greatest plastic surgeons of the time in France and Italy.

While abroad, he developed a whole new set of instruments for performing plastic surgery on the nose. This was so unusual for a young man just starting in the field that the publicity got back to the United States. One of his former professors at Columbia wrote and asked: "Are you studying or teaching over there?"

After he finished his training, Dr. Maltz returned to the United States and opened an office on lower Fifth Avenue. A week passed without a single patient coming in. The second and third weeks went by and still no patients. By then, he was beginning to get nervous. The occasional phone calls he received were from relatives who did not help his state of mind because they agreed with his father that he was not showing good sense in choosing to specialize in a form of surgery practically unknown and for which there was obviously no market.

During the fourth week, a classmate of his from Columbia brought in a prospective patient, a shoe salesman with a smashed nose. Dr. Maltz examined the man and suggested that he enter the hospital for immediate surgery. But the salesman was afraid of an operation, and he left without making a decision. For several days, Dr. Maltz's classmate worked on the man until he finally assured him that the operation was relatively simple and painless. At last, Dr. Maltz's practice was off to a rocky start.

Plastic surgery was so new then that even doctors had little idea of its possibilities. Dr. Maltz started on a campaign to inform them about his specialty. He gave talks at medical meetings. He circulated among the doctors in the hospital to which he was attached. The ear, nose, and throat men were particularly interested. Finally, they agreed to assemble a number of clinical cases to see what he could do.

They picked five of their most difficult cases, patients with terrible deformities. Six doctors in mask and gown attended the operations as observers. He was probably wrong, but Dr. Maltz says that he felt at the time that these physicians were so skeptical that they actually wanted him to fail.

But, of course, he got excellent results, and those cases led to others. He started getting more and more referrals. "I did a case here and a case there," he says. "And the most fantastic thing happened. By the end of the year, I was a success."

His international reputation came slowly. When he moved his offices to his present location at 57 West 57th Street in Manhattan, he met Dr. Frederick Alby, world famous orthopedic surgeon, who also had offices there. The two became close friends, and Dr. Alby referred many patients to him and introduced him to many other famous physicians. He began getting patients from out of this country.

He operated on the daughter of Trujillo, then President of the Dominican Republic. While there, he performed the first operations in that country on harelips and cleft palates. The results were so phenomenal that he became a celebrity. He met all the ambassadors to the Dominican Republic, and many of them induced him to come to their own countries where plastic surgery had never been performed.

Over the years, he has also performed hundreds of operations on the stars of stage, screen, and television. It's no more unusual today for a well-known personality to have a nose changed, a face lifted, or ears corrected than it is for one to have his teeth capped. "I can assure you," Dr. Maltz says, "that those who look so well on your television screen are either extremely lucky, or they have been to plastic surgeons."

From the very beginning of his practice, he was sensitive to the influence that external looks have on a person's life. "Too many people," he says, "think that they can judge character by facial appearance. They persist in considering certain features or aspects of the face as indications of character. They associate weakness of will with a receding chin, and determination with a well-developed one; stupidity with a sloping forehead or large ears; age with wrinkles and white hair; lust with thick lips."

Because of the nature of his work, he was able to observe at close range the serious handicap that abnormality, whether due to congenital or acquired defects, can impose on a person's life. It frequently destroys his happiness and endangers his chance for economic survival. In his book on the subject, *New Faces—New Futures*, he cites numerous examples of the happiness and improved economic circumstances that skillful plastic surgery has brought to the lives of many people.

Dr. Maltz himself has, through his surgery, rehabilitated hundreds of men and women who, according to their own testimony, had been forced by society into a life of crime because of facial deformities. He was instrumental in starting in New York a program of corrective surgery on criminals selected from reform schools and prisons. These criminals are all victims of facial disfigurements. Juvenile first offenders are given primary consideration. The cases chosen run the gamut from ugly depressed saddle noses to hooked beaks, cauliflower ears, harelips, or scars caused by accidents or knife wounds.

Throughout his career as a plastic surgeon, he has been a daring, creative innovator. Even as early as 1936, he introduced new methods of doing rhinoplasty (plastic surgery on the nose). He has invented new ways of skin grafting and many other new procedures. During World War II, when many servicemen—victims of the German land mines—were brought into hospitals, he invented a successful technique of reconstructing the penis.

Dr. Maltz was born with two other talents which were destined to overshadow even his illustrious career as a plastic surgeon. He is a great writer and an incredibly effective public speaker. He has the enviable ability of being able to nudge the minds and emotions of his readers and listeners. He is not only lucid, original, and logical; he is moving. When he writes and speaks, he emanates the peculiar mystique that changes people's lives.

Even when he first started writing books about his chosen field of plastic surgery, he sounded less like a doctor than a professional writer. He avoided the typical jargon of his profession. A textbook he wrote on rhinoplastic surgery has been read by as many laymen as doctors. His other books in the field are as interesting as their titles: *Rebuilding Character Through Plastic Surgery, The Long and Short of It,* and *Cyrano's Dream.*

Soon, he branched out into writing novels and plays. Among his eleven books are *Goddess with the Golden Eye, The Miracle of Dr. Fleming, The Private Life of Doctor Pygmalion,* and *The Face of Love.* Two of his many plays appeared on Broadway. One of them ran for six months; the other didn't have a chance because it opened and closed during a newspaper strike. His latest play, *Somewhere to Go,* is a comedy that reflects his philosophy on how to get more living out of life, a philosophy that he wrote about in his most famous book, *Psycho-Cybernetics.*

The concept of psycho-cybernetics evolved gradually in Dr. Maltz's mind. His *Rebuilding Character with Plastic Surgery* was the first thing written that shows the psychological, social, and economic effects of scars. Time and again, he was made aware of the happiness and new lease on life that his surgery brought to many of his patients. But sometimes, he would have a patient who did not react in the expected pattern. He would heal the outer scars, but the patient would continue to act as if the scar were still there. He or she would remain withdrawn, tense, unhappy, or whatever the preoperative psychological symptoms had been.

One notable patient was a young woman whose left cheek

had been disfigured in an automobile accident. Dr. Maltz operated on her and, to his satisfaction at least, restored her beauty. When he removed the bandages, he held a mirror up for her to see that the deformity had been removed. She looked at her image with apathy and said: "I don't see anything different."

Her obviously sincere but unexpected reaction aroused Dr. Maltz's curiosity. He started probing into her background. He discovered that the girl had been engaged to a young man who, shortly before the wedding, ran off and married someone else. The event had fractured the girl's ego, and she began thinking that she was a nobody. When she was later disfigured in the automobile accident, she accepted it almost as her due.

This case preyed on Dr. Maltz's mind. He began recalling other patients who had reacted negatively to successful plastic surgery. It dawned on him that these people had inner scars which his knife could not remove, scars caused by their own destructive self-images.

He coined the word *psycho-cybernetics* to indicate that a person's self-image automatically, without his volition, steers him to predestined action. The word *cybernetics,* as used in manufacturing, refers to any servomechanism that steers mechanical or electronic systems to desired goals. Psycho-cybernetics is the human phenomenon of a person's self-image forcing him to conform to whatever that self-image may be.

If, for example, a person starts believing that he can't cope with mathematics, he'll prove that he can't whenever an occasion arises. In the same way, if a salesman becomes convinced that he is mediocre, he will turn away from opportunities that would prove otherwise. It's like the power of imagination. If you imagine someone is following you on a dark street, your heart will beat faster. If you imagine it is cold, you will shiver. If you imagine you are sick, you are.

People who have destructive self-images have developed inner scars that are propelling them to destructive goals. The reasons may be myriad: a conflict, a heartache, a misfortune, tension, a resentment, an injured ego, a feeling of inferiority because of some error or blunder they have made. But whatever the reason, they are committed to unhappiness unless they can dig deep within themselves and remove the scars they have put there.

Dr. Maltz developed ways to help people perform their own plastic surgery on their inner scars. A famous professor of psychiatry has said that "this represented the first real breakthrough of understanding the neurosis and various psychoneurotic aspects of people who live under tension in our modern phrenetic times."

His experiments proved that positive thinking really works, but it is only of value to people who are positively oriented. They also proved it isn't necessary, as Freudians thought, to go back through a long and painful psychoanalysis to the root of a problem. All that is needed is to realize that there is a problem and to take action to do something about it.

"Once you change your image to a positive one," says Dr. Maltz, "you have kinetically tried to improve yourself. And once you have tried, you're there."

Although he agrees that financial success is within the realm of possibility to any human being who trains properly for it, his emphasis in psycho-cybernetics goes beyond mere financial success. He thinks that, to be happy, people must be successful as human beings.

At its core, Dr. Maltz's prescription for treating inner scars is through having compassion for one's self. On the Mike Douglas television show, he used the following acronym to show how to be successful as a human being, not only within yourself, but as part of a family, part of a community, part of a country, and part of the whole world:

S—*Sense* of direction. A sense of your own direction and a sense of direction that others are taking.

U—*Understanding.* This means understanding your needs and the needs of others.

C—*Courage.* You must have the courage to be honest with yourself and others.

C—*Compassion.* This refers to compassion not only for others but also for yourself, even though you have made mistakes in the past.

E—*Esteem.* You must have self-respect before you can find happiness.

S—*Self-acceptance.* You accept yourself for what you are, not blindly or with false pride but with appreciation.

S—*Self-confidence.* You get self-confidence by remembering some success of the past when you acted confidently. This will help you forget any setbacks on the way to your chosen goal.

Like all great truths, Dr. Maltz's treatment for self-fulfillment seems almost too simple to be effective. But it worked such miracles in the lives of the people with whom he dealt that he felt compelled to write a book on the subject.

The book wasn't easy to write because it was exploring and opening new frontiers of the mind. It took him years of writing and rewriting before it was finished to his satisfaction. But the end result is a beautifully written work that immediately gained widespread acceptance. For the first time in its history, the *Reader's Digest* devoted two issues of its book section to the condensation of one book. Critics gave the book glowing reviews. First the churches, then industry, then educational institutions started applying its principles.

Psycho-Cybernetics was published in 1960. Since then, it has sold 1,700,000 copies in the English language editions. With foreign publications, the number of copies in print is probably close to double that figure. In many respects, the book has radically changed Dr. Maltz's life.

He now travels about 50 percent of the time, delivering lectures, appearing on radio and TV interview shows, conducting seminars in psycho-cybernetics. He has started courses in the subject for innumerable diverse groups. For example, at Lake Orion, about forty-five miles from Detroit, there is a rest home for Catholic priests who are alcoholics. The director of that institution uses *Psycho-Cybernetics* as the basis for a rehabilitation program for those unfortunate priests. They read the book, discuss and study it in regularly scheduled classes. The results have been so spectacular that the Church is opening a similar institution in Rochester, Minnesota.

Many religious leaders say that Dr. Maltz has added a new dimension to religion. He make religion more palatable to the average man because he explains religion in a different way. He makes people stop the destructive practice of atoning for not being better than they are.

He is a member of the teaching faculty of Purdue University. The Life Insurance Marketing Institute there uses his book as a text, and each year he conducts the sessions. Results have been so successful that Hal Nutt, the director of the Institute, has become one of Dr. Maltz's most enthusiastic supporters. Through Hal's efforts, Dr. Maltz has been invited to address hundreds of sales executives' organizations.

Children also have profited from *Psycho-Cybernetics*. Its principles are taught in a number of schools now. At the

Forsythe School in St. Louis, for example, young children are taught to develop self-esteem through techniques developed by *Psycho-Cybernetics*. If a child makes a mistake, he is taught to look upon it as natural. When he succeeds in something, he is taught to register the event on his conscious mind, so that he will know that he has the seeds of success within himself.

Dr. Maltz is also becoming one of the most popular speakers on college campuses. His message is particularly applicable for the typical college student who thinks that the college is trying to reduce him to a computer statistic. Recently, Dr. Maltz addressed eleven classes in a southern university, ten of them via closed circuit television. The college president invited him because he felt that the students had no desire to learn. His speech said in substance:

> Everyone has a desire to live and be happy. If that's your goal, you will try to make something worthwhile of yourselves while you're putting in your time here in college, not just cram to get a degree and be one of twenty thousand peas in a pod. It's up to you to fulfill yourself as a human being.

He was later told that, when he finished, the students in the closed circuit classrooms stood and applauded. It is recognition of the universal need for personal dignity and self-respect that has special significance for the current crop of college students.

The philosophy of psycho-cybernetics is spreading. In 1968, thirteen-week courses in the subject were launched in major urban areas. In addition, a home study course in psycho-cybernetics, geared for people who cannot conveniently attend regularly scheduled classes, is being offered.

Eventually, Dr. Maltz thinks that psycho-cybernetics will become a required course at all levels of education. "Our greatest asset," he says, "is our dignity and self-respect. We keep saying that this is the land of opportunity. But we must stop teaching that opportunity knocks. It never knocks. You can listen at the door for ten lifetimes, but you won't hear it knocking. *You* are opportunity. You open the door."

John Kluge

J ohn Kluge waits in his Park Avenue office in stockinged feet while his shoes are sent down to be shined. He has an ingrained aversion to having a man kneel at his feet.

Kluge's acute sensitivity to the feelings of others can probably be explained by the problems he experienced as a child immigrant. He was eight years old when his family moved here from Germany. Barely able to cope with the language, his first year in an American public school proved to be a trying experience. Children can be cruel, and his classmates taunted him unmercifully, making him feel like an outsider. Since that time, he has been unusually sympathetic to the feelings of people around him.

And yet most of us who know John agree that he is a totally competitive man. He seems obsessed with being the biggest and the best. He never reaches a level that satisfies himself. Each time he achieves a hard-fought objective, he pours everything that he has accumulated into a new fraught-with-risk gamble.

His first full-time job serves as an example of how he dares to take off-trail approaches. He had just worked his way through four years at Columbia University with no outside financial help except for a four-year honor scholarship. He had no money to go into business for himself, but he was convinced that he could never fulfill his maximum potential if he became hired help. After assessing this situation, he offered to work for Otten Brothers of Detroit for a very low salary. His condition: that he be given a share of the business if he could double the company's sales.

When he made this proposition, Kluge had had no experience in the Otten Brothers' business, which was converting old envelopes and filing cards into usable paper. Besides, he had no savings to tide him over. But to the credit of the two owners, they recognized that they were dealing with an unusual person. They accepted his proposal and hired him.

Kluge, starting in the stockroom, set out to learn how to do every job in the company. He frequently worked twenty hours a day, seven days a week. Before long, he was a key man in the company. Within three years, he had achieved his goals. He had doubled sales, he was a vice-president, and he owned a third of the stock.

When he was inducted into the Army as a private in 1941, John sold his interest in Otten Brothers. Although he didn't know what he wanted to do after the war, he knew that he had to try to accomplish something really significant. It wasn't a question of money; money has never interested him except as a symbol of achievement. So when he received his honorable discharge as a captain in 1945, he began searching for something big enough to absorb his interest and talents. At the time, he did not realize that he would flit in and out of half a dozen industries within the next twenty years, making his mark in each and then moving on to look for new and bigger risks.

His first postwar venture, and one which in its own small way set the stage for the present communications complex that he heads, was into daytime radio. Fired with enthusiasm by a *Wall Street Journal* article on the profit potential of radio, he and a boyhood friend teamed together to build their own AM broadcasting station in Silver Spring, Maryland. Although his friend, Joe Brechner, had had some radio experience with the Veterans Administration, neither man knew much about the intricacies of getting a license from the Federal Communications Commission or the problems of building a station from the ground up. On the basis of articles they had read, they estimated that it would take about $15,000 to get into the business. Before the station was to get on the air, they had to raise $75,000 more than this budgeted figure. Their exploits of trying to get WGAY in operation were so wildly improbable that Joe Brechner authored the story for *The Saturday Evening Post*.

In the month before WGAY began operations, Kluge single-handedly sold $50,000 of airtime to advertisers in the District of Columbia market. From the beginning, the station was financially a success, due chiefly to John's and Joe's razzle-dazzle promotions. The station gave away prizes to attract a large, faithful audience and cooperated in community ventures to gain the reputation of operating in the public interest. It grossed more than $200,000 in its first year.

Before long, John had exhausted the potential of a daytime radio station. Unwilling to relax and enjoy the not inconsiderable income he was earning, he once again began his restless pursuit of new ways to challenge his time and energy.

For his next venture, he moved to Boston where he was the sole New England distributor of Fritos, a corn-chip snack that was gaining widespread acceptance in the South. True to form, he inaugurated a vigorous promotional campaign to introduce Fritos in his franchised territory. By such methods as putting free samples in every shopping bag that checked through supermarket counters, he gained 100 percent chain-store distribution for the brand in the first eight months.

Within a year, he had forty trucks covering his territory. He had added to his line a cheese product called Chee-tos and a Mexican snack called Pep-it-tos. Three years later, by the time he was looking around for a new challenge, he was doing over $1 million volume with such diverse lines as books, records, candies, shoe polishes, and coffee. In all, he was handling about thirty-five different products.

From this experience with the distribution of food products, John Kluge gained insight into food brokerage. At the time, most food brokers were not as imaginative as now. They reaped the rewards of commissions on the products they handled, but, to John's way of thinking, they were not taking advantage of the promotional possibilities inherent in the close relationships they held with clients. John moved back to the District of Columbia area and became a food broker.

He opened offices that became the talk of the industry. Original paintings hung on the walls. The furnishings and decor were plush, modern, and comfortable. He installed a fully equipped kitchen supervised by a first-rate chef. Each time he introduced a new product, he invited buyers and had them sample the wares direct from his kitchen during a luncheon.

The wildest promotion he pulled in those days was with a dill pickle line. When he ran an ad in the local newspaper for dill pickles, he mixed the essence of pickle with the printing ink. In this way, the readers smelled the pickles at the same time they read the advertisement. This kind of showmanship paid off. Within a few years, the firm was grossing over $10 million, and he began looking around for someone to free him from the day-to-day operations. He merged with David Finkelstein, a Baltimore food broker.

Today, Kluge, Finkelstein & Co. is one of the leaders in the industry. John as a sideline also imports coffee which provides him with a sizable income.

By 1958, Kluge was a multimillionaire and had money pouring in from half a dozen sources. Besides those mentioned, he owned a company that had the exclusive rights to distribute a silver polish made by the International Silver Company; he owned several radio stations, a TV station, and two printing companies; he owned real estate in every location in which he had business interests. By then, he felt ready to try his management skills in the big league. He began looking for a publicly held company into which to throw his resources.

When he, with the help of some close friends, bought 24 percent of Metropolitan Broadcasting Corporation from Paramount Pictures, he was gambling that he could turn the fortunes of a company with a miserable history of operations. Of its two radio and two television stations (WTTG-TV in Washington, D. C., WNEW and WABD-TV in New York, and WHK in Cleveland), only WNEW radio was profitable WABD-TV, which became WNEW-TV, had lost its network affiliation, had a history of unprofitable operations, and was $500,000 in debt. The parent company was $3 million in debt.

The turnabout in nine years of Kluge management has been breathtaking. The corporation he heads is now the umbrella for the leading independent radio and television broadcaster in the country, the leading outdoor advertising company, the leading transit advertising company, and among the leading independent television and motion picture producers. Besides, it operates a popular ice show and a rapidly growing direct-mail advertising company. It even owns the top of a California mountain. The whole concept that Kluge has exploited is so new that he had to invent the word "metromedia" to describe it. In 1961, he changed the company name to Metromedia, Inc., meaning a company that provides multimedia advertising services in major urban areas. And the corporate name is so descriptive it can encompass any other acquisitions in the media, service, or leisure activity field.

Every time John picks up a new medium, observers think that he has finally blundered. And it's true, his acquisitions from a superficial point of view do not always make sense. But as soon as he gets in the management seat, he guides the new company in a direction that can only be described as ingenious. Again and again, he has demonstrated that, in spite of the quickness with which he makes decisions to buy companies that appear to be in desperate straits, his mind has already blocked out a way to turn these sleepers into winners.

When, for example, Kluge bought the two television and two radio stations that made up Metropolitan Broadcasting Corporation, he saw promising trends in broadcasting that the untutored eye would overlook. He saw that the network stations, particularly in major urban centers, were starting to provide an umbrella for independent stations because of their gradual increases in advertising rates. He also observed a growing tendency among national advertisers to concentrate their advertising appropriations in major markets. His initial plan, then, was to capitalize on these trends—to beef up each station's operations so it could compete successfully with the networks and to embark on an expansion program in major metropolitan areas.

Metromedia now has television stations in New York, Los Angeles, Kansas City, Washington, D. C., and San Francisco. They offer a varied diet to viewers, ranging from professional football, basketball, and golf tournaments to discussions on public affairs featuring such provocative personalities as Joe Pyne, Les Crane, Louis Lomax, David Susskind, Alan Burke, and Merv Griffin.

The six AM and six FM radio stations are separate entities located in New York, San Francisco–Oakland, Los Angeles, Baltimore, Cleveland, and Philadelphia. On them, Kluge has introduced everything from stereo broadcasting to stimulating, all-talk radio, which has created unique listener involvement.

Kluge has studiously avoided equity financing in raising money for expansion. He relies on borrowing power with banks and lending institutions. And, as a result of the improved operations that he has been able to effect, his stockholders have gained tremendously from these leveraged situations. The Metromedia stock, which never sold for more than $10 a share six years ago, now sells for approximately five times that amount. Stockholders equity has soared from $10 million to $54 million.

When John Kluge purchased Foster & Kleiser, the outdoor advertising division of W. R. Grace and Company, many people again thought that he was making a mistake. Outdoor advertising as an industry was at an all-time low. The big sprawling company, operating in 400 markets, seemed to have little chance to do a turnabout. The relationship between broadcasting and outdoor advertising seemed tenuous, at best. But Kluge walks to the beat of a different drummer. He cut the operation to 28 key markets, selling off the remaining 372 properties for $8 million. He reduced the branch offices from ten to three. To streamline for greater efficiency, he reduced the personnel by 50 percent.

He ended up with 18,000 advertising panels worth $20 million. Originally, he had paid only a net of about $6 million for the company. After taking a fast depreciation in the first years, he in effect acquired a valuable outdoor advertising business and put money into his pocket at the same time. Moreover, he had a second advertising medium to offer in the major urban markets of the country. Later, he purchased

General Outdoor Advertising's New York and Chicago plants, thereby ending up with the largest outdoor advertising company in the country.

Another purchase that didn't make sense at first was the top of Mt. Wilson in California. Since his TV and radio antennas were there, even a casual observer could have understood why he might buy an acre or two on top of this mountain. But Kluge bought 720 acres that could then best be described as unproductive.

True to form, he knew exactly what he was doing. His short, intermediate, and long-range plans for the property were clearly fixed in his mind. He predicted that in due time he would receive a 100 percent return on his investment. The top of the mountain provided an immediate source of rental income because NBC's affiliate in Los Angeles, along with others, leased a few acres for its antenna. Eventually, Kluge sold the site to that station, and continued to lease the others.

The company that sold the property to Kluge had been charging twenty-five cents a head to visitors who wanted to ascend the mountain to see the view. Over 100,000 a year were paying this tariff when Kluge took over. Since the mountain is within thirty minutes of downtown Los Angeles and provides a magnificent view of the surrounding area, John realized that the number of visitors could be appreciably increased with promotion and beautification. He began an ambitious project which eventually converted the area into a scenic park intended for family recreation and relaxation. In 1967, Mt. Wilson Skyline Park was formally opened.

In Kluge's words, "The long range plan is that we will probably bring water in and develop the top of the mountain. After all, it's only eighteen miles from the heart of Los Angeles, one of the great views in the world, in one of the great growth cities of the world."

Sometimes, John's acquisitions seem so far out that it's hard even for his closest associates to explain them in terms of an integrated service approach. Anyone can now see how television stations, radio stations, an outdoor advertising company, a transit advertising company, and a mail-marketing company tie together. When these services are concentrated in the same metropolitan areas, they provide a multimedia package to advertisers, and one service can feed and complement others. Logically, the next step for Metromedia, Inc., was to expand into publishing. And, indeed, the company did just that by acquiring *Playbill* magazine and Argyle Publishing Corp.

However, it's not so clear how Ice Capades and Wolper Productions fit into the pattern. Both, of course, have sold productions to the national television media. And both are often promoted by Kluge's advertising media—via radio, TV, billboards, and transit ads. The consumers, though, are entirely different: in one instance, the consumers are business firms; in the other, the consumers, for the most part, are the general public.

Kluge explains that Ice Capades and Wolper Productions are in the live entertainment and leisure-activity field. In this respect, they are directed at servicing the same ultimate consumers as his communications activities. Looked at from this broad viewpoint, Mt. Wilson Skyline Park also fits into the pattern. But so would the ownership of any form of entertainment, from a professional hockey team to a ski area.

However, whether it's rationalizing to try to explain Metromedia's holdings as a logical extension of the company name is immaterial. What is important is the fact that the holdings make good sense financially. Ice Capades, for example, is doing sensationally well. Two separate units now perform in sixty cities in the United States and Canada, each year establishing a greater all-time high for receipts and attendance.

Every year the show appears on a network television hookup. The international company performs in Canada, Australia, Moscow, and London. A division of the company is establishing ice skating centers in major metropolitan areas.

Wolper Productions, Inc., is also enjoying a phenomenal growth. The company is the foremost producer of television documentaries and specials. Each year a growing number of its high-quality productions appear on all three television networks. Some of its recent notable documentaries have been *The Undersea World of Jacques-Yves Cousteau, The Making of the President,* and *The National Geographic Specials.*

Wolper Productions has also branched out, going into industrial films and full-length motion pictures. Among its industrial clients are General Motors, Bank of America, and the U. S. Army. Its initial motion picture production starred William Holden in *The Devil's Brigade,* and among ten other movies on its schedule is William Styron's best-selling *The Confessions of Nat Turner.*

Several years ago, Theodore Levin wrote a piece in the *Harvard Business Review* with the provocative title, "Marketing Myopia." His article has become a classic. Levin made the point that most companies take a shortsighted view of the industry they are in. The railroads, he pointed out, historically have thought that they are in the railroad rather than the transportation industry. Their shortsightedness explains their present sick condition. Logically, they should have expanded into the trucking and airline industries. Consider, for example, how different the condition of the New Haven Railroad would be if it had developed trucking and air services as an obvious part of its growth.

In the context of Levin's "marketing myopia" theory, John Kluge's broad approach to providing services to the new leisure class reflects insights that are advanced and sophisticated. He has established a competitive edge that will keep him ahead of the pack for years to come.

In 1966, he acquired three of the country's leading direct-mail and sales-promotion companies: Dickie-Raymond, Inc., O. E. McIntyre, Inc., and Sampson-Hill Corporation. He then formed them into a compact Metromail Group. With these organizations as a base, Metromedia now offers national advertisers diversified direct-mail services hitherto unavailable.

If John had allowed these new companies to follow the direction they were going when he acquired them, they would probably stir up very little interest or sensation in the advertising world. But he has a genius for reorienting the objectives of companies of which he is in command. Right now, he is embarked on a program to gear these companies to offer a direct-mail listing service that goes far beyond any currently offered. He is convinced that the computer has opened the door to a new era in which prospects can be pinpointed to a degree hithertofore undreamed of.

Each time John Kluge embarks on new, ambitious programs, he necessarily generates a certain amount of furor in his organization. Change never takes place without some internal upheaval. And in a company that's committed to change as much as Kluge's, one would expect to find a great many bitter and insecure employees. Amazingly, this is not true of Metromedia. His employees to a man are enthusiastic Kluge supporters. Part of the reason for this lies in the type of people with whom John has surrounded himself. They tend to be young and highly educated. They are real pros who welcome challenge and responsibility. John prides himself for paying top dollars for the best men he can find. And when they come with him, he gives them free rein. His executive staff consists of only seventeen people. But any one of them is capable of and willing to make top-level policy decisions.

One incident serves as a good example of his confidence in the people with whom he surrounds himself. On a trip to California, he heard that Frank Sinatra's palatial Beverly Hills home was for sale. Needing a west coast home base at the time, he instructed his lawyer to look into the matter, and proceeded on to San Francisco. While there, he received a call from the lawyer who said that the home was a good buy. The asking price was $250,000. Although he had never even seen the house, Kluge told the lawyer to go ahead and buy it.

In such a permissive environment, one can appreciate why Kluge's staff and workers admire and respect him. They talk about him constantly, and anyone within the company you buttonhole has his own theory on the secret to Kluge's success. They are all somewhat in awe of him, but as much for his unexpected humility as for his total dedication to the company and his marketing foresight.

Such respect is edifying to observe in this age when so many successful businessmen are regarded with cynicism and even hatred. It proves that success has not spoiled John Kluge. Besides being an achiever, he's a very sensitive, thoughtful human being.

James F. O'Neil

At pivotal points in his career, Jim O'Neil has turned down jobs that might have led to fame and fortune. It isn't that he wouldn't like to attain such goals. He was simply needed for more useful but less remunerative work. Jim has dared to be different by devoting his life first to the service of his community and now to the service of war veterans.

In 1934, Governor John G. Winant of New Hampshire asked Jim O'Neil to become the state's Commissioner of Labor. The Governor pointed out that this was a key post that could lead to national and international honors.

At the time, Jim was city editor of *The Union and Leader* in Manchester, New Hampshire. As a newspaper man, he was in an excellent position to move into the Commissioner of Labor's job. He knew practically all of the leading citizens of the state, and his reputation for honesty and fair play was unquestionable. But before he had time to make up his mind about the Governor's offer, Jim was recommended by the retiring Chief of Police of Manchester to take over his job. He also received a telegram from Frank Knox, the publisher of the paper Jim worked on, urging him to take the police position.

Jim had no ambition to be Chief of Police. In many respects, being city editor was more important. Other than what he had learned as a newspaper reporter, he had no experience to equip him to be police chief. But his considerations had to go deeper than his own wants. At the time, this post was causing a division among the leaders of the city and state. The job was supposed to be removed from politics because the Chief of Police was named by a three-man commission appointed by the Governor. But the incumbent Chief of Police had been in office for fifty years. He and the present Governor were not friendly toward one another. Nor were Winant and Frank Knox friendly because they had opposed one another for the Republican nomination for governor. If Jim did not take over the job, the other person being considered would cause an even deeper split among the political factions.

Jim talked the matter over with Governor Winant, and relates, "The Governor finally said to me, 'This is probably the best thing for you to do.' I reluctantly agreed to become police chief."

One of the interesting aspects of his thirteen-year tenure as Manchester's Chief of Police is the legal education that Jim acquired. In functioning as head of the police department, he had to present all cases in the juvenile and municipal courts. He also had to assist the county and state prosecutors in the upper courts. As a result, he became a specialist in the criminal statutes and code.

Three of the most widely publicized cases in which he was involved had religious overtones. Two of them reached the United States Supreme Court. These two involved the Jehovah's Witnesses. One came about because of a parade without a permit, the other because of the sale of literature in the streets without a license.

The attorney representing the Jehovah's Witnesses was Hayden Covington who was later to represent more than four

thousand of the cases involving Jehovah's Witnesses heard
before President Truman's Amnesty Board of which Jim
O'Neil was a member. Covington also represented Cassius Clay
when he used his ministerial status in order to avoid military
duty.

The Supreme Court upheld the Manchester, New Hampshire
ordinances in both instances. The Jehovah's Witnesses were required to pay the fines fixed by the New Hampshire courts.

The third case started with a fire in the combined parish
house and church of a Polish Bishop. The Bishop was out of
town the night of the fire. Because of the suspicious nature of
the fire, Jim O'Neil ordered an investigation to determine its
cause. In an upstairs hallway of the house, a wide floorboard
had been removed and about three hundred candles had been
placed between the ceiling below and the flooring above. Some
of the candles had melted, but a few had not burned, apparently because the board had snuffed them out when it was
replaced.

When the Bishop returned the following day, Jim questioned
him. The Bishop, of course, denied having anything to do with
the cause of the fire. However, a screwdriver, which had been
used to pry up the board in the hallway, was found in the
trunk of the Bishop's car. The screwdriver had left indentations in the wood; the indentations matched the width of the
screwdriver perfectly. In addition, laboratory reports proved
that wax found on the heels of the Bishop's shoes came from
the melted wax found under the flooring. Jim arrested the
Bishop for arson.

When the news broke that a Bishop had been jailed, Police
Chief O'Neil became an unpopular man. Many people equated
the Bishop with the Roman Catholic Church, and the Bishop
helped to foster this opinion in every way he could. In the first

trial, the jury was eleven to one for conviction. The holdout took the position that a priest could not possibly do the things attributed to the accused.

In the second trial, the Bishop was convicted and sent to prison for five years. Not only was he found guilty, but he was also caught in an outright lie. When asked if he, as a priest, was living under the vow of chastity, he said he was. However, Jim had conducted a painstaking investigation of the Bishop's background and these findings were the Bishop's undoing. The Bishop, Jim found, had started his career as a butcher in St. Louis. He was not a member of the Roman Catholic Church. He was really self-ordained and identified himself with the Holy Trinity National Catholic Church. Moreover, he had been married. A newspaper photograph taken of the wedding was produced as proof.

Just prior to and during most of World War II, Frank Knox, Jim's former boss on the Manchester *Union and Leader*, was Secretary of the Navy for Franklin Delano Roosevelt. In 1942, Knox asked Jim to give up his job as police chief to run for Congress. But Jim did not want to be a Congressman at that time; he wanted to get into the armed forces. He asked Knox to get him into the Navy. Knox turned him down on the ground that Jim could better serve the nation in police matters. Jim then tried to get into the Air Force, but Knox blocked that move too.

In April, 1944, Knox died. Shortly thereafter, another long-time New Hampshire friend of Jim's, John L. Sullivan, was appointed Assistant Secretary of the Navy for Air. Two days after Sullivan got the job, Jim O'Neil was attached to the Navy. Three days after that, he was in Pearl Harbor. Mr. Sullivan became Secretary of the Navy when Mr. Forrestal was named Secretary of Defense.

Jim's title was special assistant to the Secretary of the Navy.

He toured the Southwest Pacific visiting most of the occupied islands. He took part in some major invasions.

In 1946, President Truman appointed Jim a member of the President's Amnesty Commission. The other members were Owen Roberts, retired Associate Justice of the United States Supreme Court, and Willis Smith, then president of the American Bar Association and later United States Senator from North Carolina. The task of the board was to review the cases of fifteen thousand draft law violators.

After the war, friends started urging Jim to run for the office of national commander of the American Legion. He had been long active in Legion work. He was a charter member of the Legion and one of the founders of the Henry J. Sweeney Post No. 2 of Manchester. In 1936, he was appointed to the Legion's National Americanism Commission. Later he became vice-chairman and then chairman of this commission.

But Jim had never been a post commander. And no one had ever become a national commander without first being a post commander. Besides, he was not a politician by trade or instinct. The only other elective office he had sought was on the school board in Manchester when he was twenty-one years old; he had been defeated by nine votes. The cost of running for the office also deterred him. If he were to wage a vigorous campaign for national commander, he would have to visit every state in the nation. He would be expected to make appearances at Legion conventions and functions so the rank and file would get to know him. Jim could not afford such a campaign, and he was reluctant to commit his friends' money on the outside chance of winning.

Some of his strong supporters decided to try to launch him as a candidate at a luncheon on January 25, 1947, in Washington, D. C., ostensibly given for Jim in honor of his wartime accomplishments. Jim was urged to attend and announce his candidacy. Although he was honored and touched by this invitation, he refused to attend the luncheon or to commit himself.

After the banquet, a delegation came to him to urge him to run. They told him of the enthusiastic support he would have. They pointed out that he couldn't delay much longer, or he would not have time to conduct an effective campaign. One of his close friends earlier that same day had said that he had heard of only one person who was not wholeheartedly in favor of Jim's candidacy—a high official who was a past commander of the Legion.

"What did he say?" asked Jim.

"He said that the American Legion is too big a job to have a cop as its head."

This statement made Jim so mad that he decided to run.

From that day until he was elected on August 31, 1947, he waged an all-out campaign. Until then, he never realized how many friends he had. Everyone seemed to step forward in his support. The Governor of New Hampshire wrote to all the governors in the country asking them to support O'Neil. The House and Senate in New Hampshire met in joint session to support his candidacy. His backing was so widespread that halfway through the first ballot at the Legion's convention the other candidates withdrew from the race. His election was unanimous.

As with everything he undertakes, Jim threw himself wholeheartedly into the job of being national commander of the Legion. In the fourteen months he served, he traveled 184,000 miles—and that was in the era before jet planes! On one tour he left home Christmas morning of one year, and did not return until June 13 of the next.

Besides addressing American Legion audiences, the job

necessitates appearances before Congressional committees, state legislatures, college and high school assemblies. Jim conferred with the President, heads of foreign governments, governors of every state, and officials at all levels.

In 1949, a delegation from New Hampshire asked Jim O'Neil to run for the United States Senate. The spokesman said, "The whole state of New Hampshire is proud of your record with the Legion, and we like your forthright stand on important issues." Jim's alternative was to remain working for the American Legion, later as publisher of its magazine.

Besides his intense interest in his work, Jim had good reasons for not wishing to run for public office. Past national commanders of the Legion have seldom been successful at winning political elections. They make too many political enemies while in office. The Legion takes strong positions on controversial issues, especially in the areas of national security and patriotism. For example, Jim, although a lifelong Republican, had during his term as national commander been highly critical of the GOP leaders of the 80th Congress because of their opposition to Universal Military Training. He had also attacked the leaders of that Congress for opposing a bill that would have given priority to veterans seeking housing.

His lack of enough money to finance his own campaign was also another reason Jim refused to run. "It is regrettable that we have arrived at a time when only a wealthy man or a person who places himself under obligation can seek public office."

But in choosing to remain with the Legion, Jim has never felt that he was taking a second-best job. Richard Nixon said to him recently: "I'm satisfied that you made the right decision when you took the job as publisher of the American Legion magazine. Your present position affords you a greater opportunity to serve than the position of a United States Senator."

Many people who are not closely associated with the Legion

do not realize the tremendous contributions that the Legion has made and is still making. For example, the Legion is responsible for the G.I. Bill of Rights. It also conducts the most comprehensive and effective youth program in the country. American Legion baseball attracts half a million boys a year. This past year, 72 percent of the rosters of major league baseball clubs were graduates of this program.

The Legion's Boys' State and Girls' State programs attract the cream of high-school students. Each year, juniors from high schools from every state in the union gather at campuses of their state universities to study civics by doing civics. Under the guidance of adult counselors who are experts in the mechanics, the students form political parties, elect their own governors, lieutenant governors, judges. They then select delegates to go to Washington, D. C., where they participate in Boys' Nation.

The Legion also sponsors an annual oratorical contest with a theme based on the Constitution and the Bill of Rights. Each year, this program attracts 350,000 boys and girls. In 1966, the boy who won the national oratorical contest was also elected president of Boys' Nation. He was a Negro from Texas.

The Legion is now developing a plan of action for the next fifty years. This may sound strange for an organization that was born to die (the original founders thought they were in a war to end all wars). But leaders of the organization are now aware that the Legion's work must go on and must stay in tune with the times. They have elected a study group, called the Task Force of the Future. The Legion realizes that most of the benefits for veterans have been achieved except for refinement or policing. The Legion's future must be concentrated on service to the community and the nation. The task force's completed report will be presented at the Legion's 1969 National Convention in Atlanta.

One of the crucial problems facing the Legion is the reception that is being accorded and will be accorded returning Vietnam veterans. This has been given priority over all other projects. The case of the veteran, especially those who will be returning to less equality than they have enjoyed in the armed forces, is regarded as the most important consideration of all. A counseling service has been established to help make veterans more competitive in our society.

When talking about the Legion's activities, Jim always stresses that he is engaged in a team effort. He is unwilling to take credit even for the general face-lifting that has been given the American Legion magazine. For he has turned it from a house organ into a general interest magazine. He recognizes that the G.I. Bill itself has developed a more sophisticated reading audience. The magazine now has better paper, better art, better layout, and a more modern format. Only eight pages now deal with internal Legion affairs. The rest of the publication is directed to problems of general interest. The magazine's influence is felt in Congress, as well as by a broad spectrum of society.

Harry Truman once said of the Legion's national commander's job: "This is the second most important elective office in the United States, next to that of President. It is a very important office, and it can be a source of great good. All of our national commanders have served with great distinction, and many have made great contributions." As publisher of the Legion's magazine, Jim is not in a position which gives him as much national publicity as that enjoyed by each successive year's national commander. But, he has already served with devotion and distinction under several national commanders; many of his friends feel that he's the Legion's elder statesman. And he's happy because he's in a position where daily he can serve veterans and their families—and his country as well.

Dr. Wendell Phillips

If I were asked to name a candidate for the title "the world's most eligible bachelor," I'd pick Dr. Wendell Phillips. He has everything a girl could possibly want: He is young, handsome, charming, colorful, and wealthy; he converses brilliantly, makes friends easily, enjoys travel, and leads an exciting life; he is on a first name basis with presidents, prime ministers, kings, and sultans.

Lowell Thomas calls Wendell a modern-day Lawrence of Arabia. An honorary member of the Bal Harith tribe in the Aden Protectorate, he is the only American who can lay claim to being an authentic Arabian sheikh. When in Aden, he dresses in a sheikh's attire and uses his adopted name, Hussein Ali Al Harithi.

Besides exploring, Dr. Phillips has gained world renown for leading several highly successful archaeological expeditions. Because of one expedition's remarkable discoveries at the forbidden site of the Queen of Sheba's capital city in Yemen, the Junior Chamber of Commerce in 1955 named him one of America's ten outstanding young men. In honor of his significant contributions in archaeology, ten colleges and universities have awarded him honorary degrees.

But what tops them all is this man's phenomenal success as a part-time businessman. He puts Horatio Alger to shame.

With no resources other than enthusiasm and self-confidence, he made his first million dollars practically overnight. *Time* magazine estimates his present worth at around $350 million.

Wendell decided to be an explorer when he was still in grade school. He began reading the lives of famous explorers, and he is now a leading authority on the subject. At the age of ten, he acquired a pistol which he carried wherever he went; he even slept with it under his pillow. In cities, he still carries a .357 Magnum Colt "Single Action Army" or "Peacemaker" inside his coat. In the field, he wears two holstered six-shooters, and practices daily to improve his quick draw. An expert shot, he can fan a Colt cowboy style.

Even before he received his B.A. degree with honors from the University of California in 1943, Wendell began work as an explorer (later he returned to Marietta College and the University of Redlands to study for advanced degrees). He joined a paleontology expedition to Arizona, and another to Utah and the Grand Canyon. He accompanied a marine zoological collection team to the New Hebrides, Solomons, Marianas, and Marshalls.

Not until 1946, however, did his special genius for doing things with a flair display itself. He learned that the University of California was organizing a scientific expedition to South Africa, and he got a job to help raise funds.

Never before or since has anyone come near his record as a fund raiser for an archaeological expedition. He was successful in getting either money or equipment from the Army, the Navy, the Air Force, and half a hundred United States corporations, including General Motors, IBM, General Foods, Goodyear, and Remington Rand. In each instance, he went to the top man in the organization to solicit aid. He received personal help from Admiral Chester W. Nimitz, Jimmy Doolittle, General Carl Spaatz, and a host of other dignitaries and business leaders. Even the late King Farouk of Egypt contributed to the expedition.

When Wendell Phillips becomes enthusiastic about a project, he is quite literally irresistible. In soliciting aid from the famous men mentioned above, most of whom he had never seen before, he seldom asked for more than sixty seconds of their time. What's more, he never took advantage of them by attempting to stay over the allotted time. It wasn't necessary. In sixty seconds, Shell Oil gave him 50,000 gallons of gasoline, GM gave him ten trucks and automobiles, the Navy gave him $57,000 to include a medical research project in the expedition's plans, the Army gave him more equipment than he really wanted to accept.

He himself led the expedition, the largest of its kind ever undertaken. Under his leadership, his group of scientists worked the length and breadth of Africa: Egypt, Sinai, Sudan, Kenya, the Congo, the Union of South Africa, Southwest Africa, Angola, Uganda, Malagasy, Tanzania, Northern and Southern Rhodesia, and Mozambique.

When he returned to the United States, Dr. Phillips created a nonprofit organization called the American Foundation for the Study of Man. Under the auspices of this foundation, he has raised funds and led almost a dozen well-known archaeological expeditions. He led a highly successful one to Sinai in 1949. In 1950, he led the first scientific expedition into Southern Arabia.

Invited by the Imam of Yemen, the 1950 expedition ventured into forbidden territory to excavate the great Circular Moon Temple located in Marib, the Queen of Sheba's capital city. Because of internal unrest, the expedition members had to abandon their equipment and flee for their lives. All this is excitingly told in Dr. Phillips' first book, *Qataban and Sheba,* which has been printed in thirteen languages and was selected by the American Library Association as one of the best books of 1955.

His latest book, *Unknown Oman,* describes some of his recent expeditions to the kingdom of Oman. This book proved interesting to me for another reason. It gave me some insights into Dr. Phillips, and helped me understand how he has been able to accomplish so much in such a short period of time. The book is the work of a man driven by the need to do whatever he undertakes better than any average person would think of trying to do. Wendell Phillips is a perfectionist, and I suspect that he can't even help himself.

Unknown Oman, as the title implies, is a description of a little-known country in the Middle East. But what a description! Wendell goes into minute detail about every aspect of the customs and problems of contemporary Oman: education, religion, marriage and divorce, slavery, the woman's place, the laws of hospitality, the prevalent diseases and methods of treating them. To write this book, Dr. Phillips had to travel more extensively in this incredibly backward country than any other person living or dead—from the foreboding Qara Mountains to the snow white capital of Muscat.

The book shows astonishing erudition. Its bibliography alone runs thirty-six pages, and the originals of works quoted are in French, German, Arabic, Italian, and English. In passage after passage, he backs up his own impressions and observations on contemporary Oman with quotations of other travelers, historians, explorers, and journalists. No reader of the book can possibly doubt that the author is the world's leading authority on Oman.

In fact, Dr. Phillips is now the economic adviser and representative of the King of Oman. It was through the sultan that he made his first million dollars. How he accomplished this feat in one ingeniously simple business transaction deserves the closest attention of all who yearn for business success.

After his expedition into Yemen, Dr. Phillips entered Oman where he met the king, Sultan Said bin Taimur. At the time, Oman was engaged in a frontier dispute with Saudi Arabia. Dr. Phillips, in a remarkable exhibition of showmanship and diplomacy, traveled to the disputed site and studied the area. Then, in the presence of representatives from both sides, he dramatically planted a stone which he proclaimed as the boundary between the two countries.

After that, Dr. Phillips and Sultan Said bin Taimur became close friends. They engaged in many discussions about the economic conditions of the country and what could be done. At one of these sessions, the Sultan suggested that Dr. Phillips take over a defunct oil concession that had been dropped by Petroleum Development, Ltd., a subsidiary of Iraq Oil Company. The concession covered the Province of Dhofar, a territory the size of the state of Indiana.

That very night, the Sultan, who is a lawyer and scholar, began writing the agreement in longhand. It begins:

> By these presents Sultan Said bin Taimur, King of Oman, grants unto the Philpryor Corporation, a company incorporated in the State of Delaware, in the United States of America, and hereinafter referred to as "the company," through their president, Dr. Wendell Phillips, the exclusive license and permission to explore and prospect for natural gas, crude petroleum and cognate substances, including asphalt, bitumen and ozokerite, in the Dependency of Dhofar in South Arabia, including the territorial waters thereof.

To a less gifted man, this concession would have been worthless. No oil had ever been found within hundreds of miles of

Dhofar. The Iraq Petroleum Company, a highly respected and successful company, had held its concession for fourteen years and then dropped it. During that time, the company had made several surveys, including a five-hundred-mile trek with a caravan of seventy-six camels. It had found nothing to make it optimistic about drilling. Dr. Phillips had nowhere near the money it would take to search for oil.

There were others problems. The country of Oman had no skilled work force, no facilities, no ports, no place for ships to dock. In fact, there were no roads to the areas where oil might be found. These areas were so remote that only a handful of explorers had even ventured into them.

But Dr. Phillips is no ordinary man. Weeks later, when he was back in Manhattan, he received the final draft of the Sultan's concession in the mail. Within hours, he was huddled at the Club 29 with W. Alton Jones, the president of Cities Service Oil Company. As usual, Wendell's enthusiasm sparked a kindred response in Mr. Jones and other officials of Cities Service. Dr. Phillips' corporation was granted a 2½ percent royalty in return for his Dhofar oil concession. His description of how the parties finally arrived at 2½ percent is a masterpiece of understatement:

"Cities Service officials countered with various proposals. But I was never good at arithmetic and by then I was really getting confused. I understood 2½ percent. I wanted 2½ percent. I didn't want any other arrangement and said so plainly. After days of apparently futile negotiations, when it was finally clear that it was 2½ percent or nothing, I received what I had asked for in the first place. Thus, it paid me not to be too clever in arithmetic."

And now comes the fantastic part of the story. At this point, Dr. Phillips had a 2½ percent royalty override on oil that might someday be dug in Dhofar. But his chances of receiving an income from this royalty were remote, to put it mildly. How could he turn 2½ percent of a possible nothing into something concrete?

He started his road to a fortune by breaking his share of the royalty in Philpryor Corporation into 1,500 units. He sold 1,000 of these units to various acquaintances for $10,000 each. In this one transaction he banked a million dollars, while still retaining a third of the royalty which could be worth $100 million more.

After a lifetime in sales work, I must point out that there isn't more than one man in a thousand who could have accomplished what Dr. Phillips did in this transaction. Because of the obstacles facing any attempt to find oil in Dhofar and then market it, most men would be content to sell out an interest in such an oil concession for a few thousand dollars, and few investors would be willing to pay more. But Wendell already had a history of accomplishing the unusual. The simple fact of his presence in the venture made it one in which highly practical businessmen were willing to invest. To me, this case is a remarkable example of success breeding success.

There's more to the story, of course. The search for oil has brought the Province of Dhofar to life. The first road has been built across the Qara Mountains which rise 4,000 feet above the Arabian Sea. About $60 million has been spent in digging wells throughout the area—many deeper than 10,000 feet. Hundreds of Arabs from Aden, Yemen, and Dhofar have been given steady employment and modern medical care for the first time in their lives.

The impact of Dr. Phillips' work in Oman and Muscat promises to be just the beginning. The Shell Oil Company of Oman has discovered oil just east of Dhofar and is already in commercial production. It is just a matter of time before Dhofar becomes productive.

Meanwhile, the Sultan is so happy with what Dr. Phillips is accomplishing in Oman that he has granted him an offshore concession extending out to a distance of 1,000 feet covering 300 miles of coastline at the entrance of the Persian Gulf. A West German oil company has taken over this concession in return for a 5 percent royalty to Dr. Phillips.

In 1965, the Sultan granted Dr. Phillips a second offshore concession covering 450 miles and running all the way to Ras Minji facing the Indian Ocean.

The kingdom of Oman is just one of many areas in which Dr. Phillips holds oil concessions or royalties on concessions. Once he got into the business, even on a part-time basis, he threw himself into it wholeheartedly. Today, he is the world's largest individual oil concessionaire with interests in every corner of the globe where development is taking place.

Fortune magazine has written a major article about Dr. Phillips. *Time* magazine has written about him many times. He is well known in Washington, D. C., especially in the upper echelons of the White House and the State Department. Among oilmen, he is one of the most talked about men around. In the Middle East, he is probably the best-known American alive. And yet, he is so little known to the average American citizen that he appeared as himself in 1967 on the television program *To Tell the Truth*.

I hope that this chapter will acquaint many more readers with this remarkable man. In an age when the pressure is on people to conform, he stands out as a shining example of what a man can do when he dares to be different. He is cast in the mold of our great American heroes.

Joan Crawford

A t first, Joan Crawford's ambition was to gain recognition as a dancer. When she succeeded in appearing in the chorus line of a Broadway musical while still in her early teens, she risked her budding career on a six months' movie option. When she became a star as a dancer in movies, she insisted on tackling difficult dramatic roles. She rose to the heights in Hollywood, achieving superstardom and an Academy Award. She has now moved on to become a famous businesswoman, and she's still a great dramatic actress. Her talent, like a good wine, improves with age.

Joan's life stands as a series of achievements, each more impressive than the last. She has dared to be different by stretching her talent to risk more demanding roles in a profession where even one mediocre performance can ruin a career.

During one period in Hollywood, Joan lived through the unhappy experience of making one motion picture after another that followed a pat formula. Each story was a variation on the Cinderella theme: a down-to-earth, poor girl rises from the slums to riches and happiness by virtue of driving ambition and indomitable courage. Oddly, Joan's own life story has been a reenactment of this hackneyed formula that almost type-cast her into oblivion.

She got off to an inauspicious start in life. Her father and mother separated before she was born. For years, she did not know that her real name was Lucille Fay Le Sueur and that she had been born in San Antonio, Texas. She was brought up with the name Billie Cassin. Her stepfather, Henry Cassin, ran a vaudeville house in Lawton, Oklahoma.

For the most part, Joan had an unhappy childhood. She recalls that her mother favored her older brother, Hal, and switched Joan's legs for anything that went wrong. Her happiest memories are of the dancers who performed in Henry's vaudeville house. She spent all her free time watching them rehearse, daydreaming of the time when she too would perform before an audience. But when she was six years old, she stepped on a piece of glass and sliced a part of her foot to the bone. The doctor who sewed the stitches said that she would never again be able to walk, run, or dance.

For a long time, it appeared as if the doctor was right. The wound reopened everytime she put weight on the foot. Finally, she became a virtual invalid, and the skin along the cut firmed and eventually healed. Two years after the accident, she was again running and dancing.

By then, however, her mother and stepfather were having a marital crisis. The problem began when Joan accidentally found several bags of money in the cellar of the house. "Daddy, it seemed, in addition to his theater, was involved in an insurance business with a partner. This partner had stolen the money, and Daddy had hidden it in fear of being held as accessory to the crime. Faced with mother's hysterics, he promised to turn the money over to the police. Hal and I were hustled off on a train to visit our Grandmother Johnson on a farm near Phoenix."

Although Henry was cleared of any complicity, Joan's mother was embarrassed by the publicity. She persuaded Henry to sell the vaudeville house and move to Kansas City where the family for a time managed a run-down hotel. But the marriage was no longer a happy one. Night after night, Joan would lie in bed listening to her mother and stepfather quarreling. Finally, Henry abandoned them.

In order to support the family, Joan's mother opened a hand laundry. They built a balcony above the washing area where Joan and her mother slept. Joan's bed was a pallet. She bathed in the laundry tubs below. In order to remain in St. Agnes Academy, a Catholic grade school, Joan made arrangements to work for her tuition. She waited on tables, washed dishes, and made beds.

When she completed St. Agnes Academy, she entered a boarding school where the arrangement was that she would again work to pay for her schooling. Her plight there was pitiful. She was kept working so hard that she had no time to attend classes. She made the beds, cleaned the rooms, cooked, and washed dishes for thirty other boys and girls. The wife of the headmaster often beat her with a broom handle. "Once she overheard me ask another girl to hand me a dustpan. She grabbed me by the hair, threw me down a flight of stairs to the basement, and beat me with the broom handle until I was dazed." Joan ran away repeatedly but always returned when she realized that she had nowhere to run. At the end of two years, the school forged credits and presented her with a high school diploma.

Joan's mother was not heartless in keeping the girl in a school where she was unhappy and claimed to be mistreated. The fact is, she had married again, and her husband did not want the girl around. "Instead of adding to the family, this man made me feel more alone than ever. Mr. Hough was moody, he seldom spoke to me. I wondered if mother really liked him. I didn't know. She was still mother, but she was living behind some glass partition I couldn't penetrate.... We lived in different worlds. She had felt sure that life would pick up for us when she married Mr. Hough. I never did tell her that I ran away finally because the one thing Mr. Hough tried to pick up was *me*."

Things were not all grim. Joan's most pleasant moments were the times she practiced dancing. During one summer vacation while she was home from the boarding school, she got a job working in the notions department of a department store. That winter, she won a dancing cup at a fraternity dance at the Jack O'Lantern Cafe in Kansas City.

Her mother did not realize how little Joan had learned in high school. In fact, she thought she had a genius on her hands because Joan had taken only two years to get her diploma. She made Joan, who was now thirteen years old, apply for entry into Stephens College in Columbia, Missouri. Joan arranged to wait on tables as payment for the tuition. She lasted in college until the first midterm exams. "The classes were Greek to me. College was only comprehensible when I was dancing...into the kitchen with a tray of dishes, into the classroom, across the campus. There were glorious dances at the University of Missouri and at the College Inn where Orville Knapp's orchestra played."

Her experience with college convinced Joan that dancing was the only competitive advantage she had as well as her most important interest in life. She decided to make a career of it. She got a job in Kline's Department Store in Kansas City and took dancing lessons. A few months later, she tried out for a chorus line in a road company. She got the job but the revue folded a week later in Springfield, Missouri. She returned to Kline's Department Store.

"Restless, energetic, I was only waiting until I'd saved enough money to make a try for the big time—Chicago. I went sooner than I'd planned. Mother and I quarreled because I came home late from a dance. I packed my bag and walked out for the last time."

When Joan got off the train in Chicago, she had four dollars. She spent two taking a taxi to the offices of Ernie Young, a theatrical booking agent. The outer office was crowded with show girls when Joan entered. For the first time, she became fully aware of the enormity of her conceit to think that Chicago would be waiting with open arms for an unknown fifteen-year-old dancer from Kansas City. She knew no one and had no real dancing credits to help her get a job.

It's moments like this that make or break people's lives. In Joan's case, she revealed an inner steel and determination that would make her the great star that she is today. She realized that she would never get a job that day unless she did something drastic. So the next time the door to Ernie Young's private office opened, she let out a scream and, with tears streaming down her cheeks, she burst into the room and confronted the startled Mr. Young: "I'm not as tall or pretty as those other girls but I have less than two dollars and no experience and I can't go back to Kansas City," she cried without introducing herself. "Please, won't you give me a tryout?" ("I played that scene again in *Dancing Lady*—pushed my way into Clark Gable's office—and one critic ridiculed it as overdone. Believe me, I didn't begin to show the desperation of the original scene.")

Her performance that day was inspired enough to move Ernie Young. He found her a job at the Friar's Inn in Chicago, where she sang and danced in eight routines a night for a week, for twenty-five dollars. From there, she landed a two-week job in Oklahoma City. Next, she moved on to Detroit.

One night in the Oriole Terrace in Detroit she whirled by a table, and her flaring gypsy skirt knocked a customer's drink in his lap. This instance proves Joan's flare for the dramatic because the customer was J. J. Shubert, who was in Detroit for an out-of-town tryout of a new musical play, *Innocent Eyes*. The play was to open on Broadway in ten days. Mr. Shubert offered Joan a job in the chorus line of his show. "Just in case the boss of the Oriole Terrace wouldn't let me go, I committed a theatrical crime. I jumped the show."

From a Kansas City dancing school to a Broadway play in twelve weeks is a big leap. But once off the launching pad, Joan's whole career has been meteoric. Before her freshman classmates were to graduate from Stephens College, she would be a motion picture star in Hollywood. Her energy was to prove as boundless as her ambition.

She loved the glamour and excitement of Broadway. While in New York, one of the best friends she made was another young dancer from the chorus of *Innocent Eyes*, Jack Oakie. She and Jack spent their afternoons together, riding buses or window shopping. "We both had great hopes for our careers. Ours was no romance. As a matter of fact, knowing Jack taught me that girls and fellows can be friends, that there is a wealth of sharing for two people who have a relationship uncluttered with coquetry."

Shortly before Christmas, Harry Rapf, producer for Metro-Goldwyn-Mayer motion pictures in Hollywood, saw a performance of *Innocent* Eyes and offered Joan a screen test. She passed the test and MGM offered her a six-month contract at seventy-five dollars a week. She accepted and took a train to Hollywood. She was seventeen years old.

Instead of being elated by her movie contract, Joan was haunted by the six-month termination clause. Her ambition had now become honed to a fine edge. She would be hard to please even with good roles. And Hollywood was a long way from offering her anything of substance. For a while, she was used simply for cheesecake photos.

"I probably had more pictures taken than any girl who'd ever been signed at the studio, because, as a dancer, I could leap the highest and jump the farthest. They also took pictures of me as I came out of a firecracker for the Fourth of July, climbing down a chimney in a fur-trimmed Santa Claus bathing suit with a Teddy bear in my pack, and in all sorts of chiffon scarfs and beads, some of the most artistic of these for European publication. Once they took me down to Seventh and Broadway in Los Angeles, put me in a traffic cop's hat and let me stop traffic. I stopped quite a bit of traffic, and that photo broke in newspapers across the country. I was in pictures, that's true, but not *moving*."

But Joan was determined to be a success. She spent her free time standing in the wings when the great stars of the time were performing. She devoted endless hours to watching William Haines and Eleanor Boardman make pictures. She spent so much time watching them that the three of them became close friends, although Joan was still an unknown. She also watched and memorized every move that stars like Marion Davies and Mae Murray made. For the first time in her life she realized that she had found a medium and a profession in which, with work, she could excel.

Her first movies never gave her a chance. In *Lady of the Night* she dubbed for Norma Shearer who was playing a dual role. In *Pretty Ladies* she was an extra. She can't even remember the part she played in her third picture. The fourth was a bit part "that Jack Conway tossed me to keep me from hounding his office."

Her first major role came as a result of her dancing. One night, Edmund Goulding, the director, saw her dancing with Michael Cudahy, heir to the Chicago packing fortune, at Hollywood's Coconut Grove. "He said that when I Charlestoned, it was as if I were intoxicated with joy. It *was* joy—I never touched liquor. I barely touched earth." Goulding offered her the role of Irene in his forthcoming production, *Sally, Irene and Mary*. The other two roles were played by Constance Bennett and Sally O'Neil.

Joan is the first to admit that her acting in these early movies was pretty bad. She says that she moved too much, cried too much, and photographed like a caricature. But what distinguished her from most of the other starlets on short-term option was her serious determination to learn and improve. She read her lines with endless variations. She pestered the director, the cameramen, and the other actors with questions. She experimented with her makeup, her eyebrows, and her hairdo. In one of her early pictures, she broke her ankle during an apache dance. "But I wanted the part so badly, I said it was *nothing*, nothing at all. My ankle was bound up, and I went on dancing."

With the release of *Sally, Irene and Mary*, Joan was tabbed as one of MGM's leading players. But she was still not satisfied. Her fierce ambition drove her to study all the harder. She played in a movie with the great Lon Chaney, the man of a thousand faces, and she was fascinated with his ability to throw himself into a role with such profound concentration that he wouldn't even emerge from it during the lunch break. From John Gilbert, in a movie they made called *Twelve Miles Out*, she learned how "to keep vitality undiluted, never to let down for a moment."

She became known as a notorious script stealer. She read every play that she could get her hands on, searching for parts that would challenge her abilities. When she found such a part, she begged for it.

One day she stole a script based on a story that was running serially in the Hearst papers. It was called *Our Dancing Daughters*. She went to the producer, Hunt Stromberg, and

pleaded with him to give her a part in the picture. He gave it
to her.

Our Dancing Daughters made Joan Crawford a Hollywood
star. Her salary was raised to five times what she had been
making. Her name from then on appeared in lights on theater
marquees. Her performances were now reviewed. Fan mail
poured in. But still, she was not satisfied. "On screen for some
time, I had specialized in carefree, blithe young girls, and like
them I had been sure of myself in a brash, juvenile way. But
now I began to doubt, study, and observe myself. I had sense
enough to know that I must work and work hard. From that
moment to this, I've kept setting the goal higher."

In her private life, Joan Crawford had met and fallen in
love with Douglas Fairbanks, Jr. At that time, he represented
everything that she had missed in her own life. "He was the
epitome of suaveness. He had had a comprehensive education
in France and England. He could write, paint, had a gay,
delicious wit, exquisite manners, and so much knowledge that
it was hard for me to reconcile his conversation with his
youth."

They married and for a while lived happily together. From
Douglas, Joan learned about poetry and books. For the first
time, she read authors like Shaw, Ibsen, Proust, and Nietzsche.
They embarked on programs of self-improvment: dancing,
music, Spanish, and French.

What finally broke them up is what broke up all three of
Joan's Hollywood marriages. She was more ambitious than her
husband. This doesn't mean that she didn't love Douglas.
She loved him and respected him. She still speaks of him
with deep affection. But with Joan, her career had to come
first. They parted friends.

Meanwhile, Joan was still fighting for good roles. No longer
satisfied with dancing roles, she demanded dramatic and emo-

tional parts. One day, she found the precise role she wanted in a script called *Paid*. It was the story of a department store clerk who had been railroaded to prison and who emerges bent on revenge.

Joan pleaded with Hunt Stromberg to give her the part. But both Stromberg and Louis B. Mayer were opposed because the role was out of character with the public image that Joan had built. Joan kept after them. She was finally given the part. In reviewing her acting, *Variety* said, "Histrionically she impresses us as about ready to stand up under any sort of dramatic assignment."

In her next picture, *Dance, Fools, Dance*, Clark Gable played a minor role. With his amazing ability to scent box office appeal, Louis Mayer observed the chemistry between Clark and Joan and put them together in a series of pictures. She and Gable became lifelong friends.

In *Grand Hotel* her costars were Greta Garbo, Lionel and John Barrymore, and Wallace Beery. ("I listened. I sat quietly, watching every actor, every nuance, every scene.")

Joan was still learning and still fighting for roles which would stretch her talent. She played opposite leading men like Gary Cooper, Robert Young, and Franchot Tone. In *Mannequin* her leading man was Spencer Tracy. In *The Shining Hour* she costarred with Margaret Sullavan, Fay Bainter, Melvyn Douglas, and Robert Young. "I spent my days in the projection room watching new movies ... I'd play Wallace Beery's grandmother if it was a good part."

Her best role at MGM at that time was *A Woman's Face*. Critics agreed that this was the finest picture to emerge from Hollywood for a long time. But Joan was unhappy with most of the pictures she was making. She finally left MGM and for three years made no pictures. Most people thought that her career was finished. But the truth was, she could not find a story that was challenging enough for her.

In 1945, she proved that she was not finished. She starred in a Warner Brothers movie, *Mildred Pierce.* The movie was based on a James M. Cain novel, produced by Jerry Wald and directed by Mike Curtiz. Her costars were Ann Blyth, Jack Carson, and Zachary Scott. Her portrait of Mildred won for her the motion picture industry's highest tribute: an Academy Award as the best actress of the year. There followed a series of great movies, all box office successes.

In 1955, Joan married Alfred N. Steele, chairman of Pepsi-Cola Company, and she left Hollywood. Joan's theory, based on three unsuccessful marriages, is that a wife, whatever interests she may have, owes the greatest part of her time to her husband's career. She decided that her acting career would be dictated solely by her responsibilities as Mrs. Steele. She began to play a new role as hostess for her husband on his worldwide travels for Pepsi-Cola.

No one who reads her autobiography, *Portrait of Joan,* can doubt that Joan had found peace and happiness in her marriage to Alfred Steele. He was someone she could look up to. His career was even more important than hers had been. And he was willing to share it with her, so she gained a whole new exciting life because of her marriage.

In 1959, less than four years after the marriage, Al Steele died of a heart attack. Although Joan was grief stricken, she realized her responsibilities to her husband's business interests. After she became the first woman member of the board of directors of the Pepsi-Cola Company, she set about carrying on his thinking in the public relations and marketing areas. She also became a member of the board of Frito-Lay, Inc. As official hostess, she literally flies around the world several times a year, making public appearances, attending ceremonies such as the opening of bottling plants, and meeting with sales groups. Her interest in sales is so keen that she is the first woman member to be inducted into the Sales Executives Club of New York.

Somehow, she has found time to return to moviemaking and television. In recent years, she has starred in such pictures as *The Caretakers, Strait-Jacket, Whatever Happened to Baby Jane?* and *Berserk,* her latest film. She has also appeared in several half-hour video dramas and television specials.

Joan lives in a Fifth Avenue duplex penthouse apartment in Manhattan, just seven minutes' ride from the headquarters of the Pepsi-Cola Company. As one would expect of a great star, the apartment is a stunning showcase. The rumor that Joan makes guests take off their shoes when they walk on her wall-to-wall white carpet is not true. But the rumor that she never appears in public unless she is impeccably groomed and beautifully dressed is true.

W. Clement Stone

When W. Clement Stone picks up a ringing telephone, he beams into the mouthpiece and explodes with bright enthusiasm: "Hi! Ter-r-r-if-f-f-ic!"

He likes the word terrific, and uses it a score of times a day. It appears in his letters, telephone conversations, conferences, speeches, even in the annual reports of his companies. If you ask Clem how he feels, he'll probably startle you by enthusiastically shouting: "I feel HEALTHY! I feel HAPPY! I feel TER-R-R-IF-F-F-IC!"

Clem Stone dares to be different because he lives by success formulas. He has spent a lifetime proving first to himself and then to others that success lies within the reach of all of us. "My aim," he says, "is to help people learn how to avoid mental illness and maintain good mental health, how to acquire wealth with the aid of self-help literature. I keep hammering away at the fact that you cannot eliminate poverty until you change the mental attitude of those who are impoverished. A good self-help book can help change the course of the life of an individual."

But before I describe the many ways that this remarkable man has helped others find success, I want to show how he himself overcame obstacles to become eventually the president and principal owner of Combined Insurance Company of

149

America and its subsidiaries—The Hearthstone Insurance Company of Massachusetts, Combined American Insurance Company headquartered in Dallas, and First National Casualty Company in Fond du Lac, Wisconsin—the chairman, president, and principal owner of Hawthorn Books, director of Alberto Culver, and the editor and publisher of *Success Unlimited*, an inspirational self-help magazine. He is the recipient of an Horatio Alger Award for having risen from rags to riches.

Clem believes that every disadvantage in our personal lives presents an opportunity in disguise if we look for it. To prove his point, he tells an anecdote about his widowed mother. Needing an income to support herself and Clem, she pawned her jewels to raise enough money to buy a small Detroit insurance agency. Her remaining cash went toward rental of desk space in a downtown building. Then, she discovered that she couldn't sell insurance. She spent fruitless days trying to close a sale. Finally, sick with fear and despair, she reached the point where she had nowhere to turn.

Clem says that she couldn't have been luckier. He is convinced that the best thing that can happen to a person is to be thrown into a desperate situation, to be faced with a serious problem with no apparent answer. In his mother's case, her desperate situation made her turn to prayer. She asked for guidance and suddenly a plan of action occurred to her. She decided that she had been calling on the wrong prospects first, that she should start with the most important person, not an unimportant one, in each office or company where she canvassed.

The next morning, she went to the largest bank in Detroit and sold a policy to the head cashier. He in turn gave her permission to sell in the bank during working hours. In this way, she made forty-four sales the day after she was ready to give up. She went on to develop a very successful insurance agency.

Clem tells about a similar situation in his own career. The time was 1939. By then he had his own insurance agency with more than a thousand licensed agents working for him in every state in the union. His contract with a large eastern insurance company was oral; it gave him exclusive distribution of specified accident policies. In effect, he owned the business and paid all expenses; the insurance company issued the policies and paid the claims.

On a fateful spring morning, he received a letter from the insurance carrier terminating his services at the end of two weeks. His and his agents' licenses were to be canceled, and no policies were to be sold or renewed after that date. Furthermore, the president of the insurance company was leaving on a trip and could not be reached before the two weeks expired.

Clem prayed for guidance just as his mother had done. He too conceived of a plan of action which he straightaway set out to accomplish. He knew that he would have to gain at least a temporary delay in the cancellation of his contracts, and the only way that he could get it would be to reach the vacationing president. He vowed to himself that, despite the difficulties and obstacles he would encounter, he would reach this man by phone that very day. For hours his long-distance phone calls led him up blind alleys. But he was relentless in his pursuit, and his determination finally paid off. When he reached the president, he was so positive and persuasive that the president agreed to continue the agency relationship as if no correspondence had transpired.

Ultimately, this ordeal was indirectly responsible for Clem's fantastic success. It made him realize that he should have an insurance company of his own. He went on to create one of the largest and most successful accident and health insurance companies in the world. He and his family have tangible wealth in excess of a third of a billion dollars, and Clem is a living testimonial to the truth of his career philosophy, which he describes in his book, *The Success System That Never Fails.*

Clem first learned that adversity can be an advantage when he was six years old selling papers on Chicago's tough South Side. He walked into Hoelle's Restaurant, a busy and prosperous place, and sold a newspaper to a diner at the first table inside the door. Almost immediately, Mr. Hoelle appeared and hustled him out the front door.

He peeked through the window and waited until Mr. Hoelle wasn't looking. Then, he hurried back into the restaurant where he sold two more papers before Mr. Hoelle once again gave him the bum's rush. Again, he entered the restaurant when Hoelle wasn't looking and again was quickly escorted out.

By now the diners were laughing heartily and enjoying the show. The next time he entered, one of them entreated Mr. Hoelle to let Clem sell his papers without interference. Within five minutes he had sold out.

When he appeared the next night, Mr. Hoelle made a half-hearted effort to throw him out and then gave up trying. From then on, as long as he sold papers, Clem Stone made Hoelle's Restaurant a regular nightly stop on his rounds.

One of the odd things about this episode is the fact that Clem was really not feeling aggressive. On the contrary, he was scared and nervous. But even at that age he realized that, if you court success, you must do the things that you're afraid to do. He now adds to this philosophy, "And do them *now.*"

For a vacation job after his second year of high school, Clem started selling insurance for his mother's agency. His first day in the field marked the beginning of a long and tireless search for the key to an airtight sales system. Like most great salesmen, he at first made his share of errors, but was wise enough to learn from them. He learned, for example, never to ask for a prospect's time but to take it. He learned that when there's a great deal to be gained and nothing to lose by trying, it's always right to try. He learned how to husband his time, the most important ingredient in any formula for successful human activity. He learned, above all, to overcome fear and timidity by taking a positive mental attitude and forcing himself to do the things that he was afraid to do.

By the time he was nineteen, he was averaging forty-eight sales a day. He decided to open his own agency in Chicago under the name of Combined Registry Company. He rented office space from a man named Richard H. Pickering who taught him that even a name has important implications. This happened when Mr. Pickering asked how he wanted his name listed on the lobby directory.

"C. Stone," he said. This was the way he then signed his name.

"What is your full name?" asked Mr. Pickering.

"William Clement Stone."

"Did you ever stop to consider that there are thousands of C. Stones? But chances are in the entire United States there is only one W. Clement Stone."

From that time on, he has signed his name "W. Clement Stone."

Almost in spite of himself, he started acquiring a sales force. He made no effort to recruit salesmen, but time after time men to whom he sold policies asked if they could represent him. His selling methods were so impressive (by then he was making as many as seventy-two sales a day for nine working days in a row) that these people voluntarily asked to become associated with him. He hired them, but he made them pay their own state license fees.

Soon he began to realize an increased income because of the override he received from the production of these salesmen. He decided to advertise for more representatives. Accordingly, he ran a four-line advertisement in the classified ad section of the Chicago Sunday *Tribune*. The ad began: "Exceptional Opportunity to Earn."

This ad resulted not only in his hiring a number of new agents in Chicago and elsewhere in Illinois, but also in his opening territories in a number of other states, including Indiana, Wisconsin, and Michigan. Before long he had over a thousand agents representing him throughout the United States.

What's remarkable about this period in Clem Stone's career is the fact that he continued to sell full-time. He hired a thousand producing salesmen whom he did not train except for giving them the few pages of mimeographed instructions to get them started. His only contact with many of them, including the branch managers he appointed in other states, was through occasional correspondence.

But he was living in a fool's paradise. Those were boom days preceding the great depression, and even mediocre salesmen could get along. By 1931, however, Clem's sales force disintegrated. Many who were still with him were barely subsisting. Finally he had to face up to the fact that they would not survive without his help. For, amazingly, Clem found selling as easy during the depression as before. He had found his success system that never fails, and he could always find opportunities where others found adversity. He has written that "the depression was a blessing in disguise for those who developed the right mental attitude."

He began indoctrinating his sales force with his self-motivating techniques. He taught them to write out their career objectives, to turn disadvantages into greater advantages, to keep a daily time evaluator. At first he planned to work only with the men who were still with him. But as these salesmen caught the fever of his infectious enthusiasm, they attracted others who wanted to join the organization. It wasn't long before Clem again had a thousand sales representatives. But this time they were, to a man, highly motivated and successful.

Clem was now a success. At this point in his career, he would probably have been happy to remain where he was, representing an Eastern insurance company, with his loose-knit agency doing business in every state. But when this was almost wrested from his control because of the whim of one of the officials in the insurance company's home office, Clem resolved to get his own company.

He realized that it would take a long time to become licensed in all the states where he had agents, so he decided to look for a going concern that already had licenses. Specifically, he wanted a company with the licenses but with little or no insurance in force. The cost of one with a great deal of insurance in force would be prohibitive.

He started a word-of-mouth campaign among his business acquaintances. To everyone he talked with, he explained that he was in the market for an insurance company, that he wanted one that was licensed in several if not all states, that the less insurance it had in force the better. He kept talking and looking for ten months before anything happened. Then he received a telephone call from one of the first people to whom he had talked about his plan to buy a company. He was told that the Commercial Credit Company of Baltimore, Maryland, was planning to liquidate the Pennsylvania Casualty Company, which had a charter to operate in thirty-five states.

All of the Pennsylvania Casualty Company's business had already been reinsured by two other insurance companies owned by the Commercial Credit Company of Baltimore.

Nothing was left except negotiable securities and cash worth $1.6 million.

Within ten minutes after he heard the news, Clem Stone was talking by long-distance phone with one of the Baltimore directors of Commercial Credit. At 2 P.M. the next day he and his attorney were at a board meeting of Commercial Credit in Baltimore. At this meeting Clem eloquently pointed out the advantages of a clean sale as opposed to liquidating the Pennsylvania Casualty Company. The directors could accomplish their objectives quickly and with certainty. Clem than offered $25,000 for the company's charter.

"But what about the $1.6 million of assets?" asked one of the directors.

"That's easy," said Clem. "Commercial Credit is in the business of loaning money. I'll simply borrow the money from you, and I'll pledge the company you are selling me as collateral."

"But when do you intend to repay the loan?" he was asked.

"I'll repay $1.1 million of it in sixty days, and the balance, which will be fully pledged, from earnings."

He knew that he needed only $500,000 to operate Pennsylvania Casualty with his own sales force. As a result, he planned to reduce the company's capital and surplus by $1.1 million. Since the assets of the company consisted only of cash, government bonds, and high-grade securities, Clem was able to do as he promised well within the sixty days.

Today, the Combined Group of Companies operates in every state of the union, in Canada, Great Britain, Australia, New Zealand, Puerto Rico, the British West Indies, and the Virgin Islands. At first, the salesmen specialized in accident and health policies. In 1966, the company entered the life insurance field. But as is to be expected, Clem Stone tried a different tack than that taken by other life insurance companies. He set his sights on earning money the first year from the sale of life insurance (historically, the writing of new life insurance develops a loss of surplus because of high selling costs). To accomplish this, he had his salesmen concentrate on relatively small sales of fixed amounts of insurance, either $1,200 or $2,400 policies. Moreover, they sold only to prospects who were already accident policyholders of the company.

What have been the results of this new venture? Clem says that it is "fantastically successful. Some salesmen have averaged as many as one hundred new life policies in a single week. We have found a formula whereby we can sell life insurance and pick up surplus annually."

The most extraordinary part about the success of Clem Stone's insurance companies is the fact that he has always specialized in selling what are known as preissue policies. Each agent, in effect, underwrites his own business. He himself issues the policies while he is in front of the prospect. No home office approval is necessary, and the policies are guaranteed renewable at the same premium as long as the insured lives. The only time the salesman has to call back is to collect another premium or to increase the coverage.

Naturally, this kind of selling situation makes a company vulnerable to unscrupulous sales practices unless the salesmen are men of integrity and motivated to render a service. An insurance salesman's income is directly related to the amount of business he does, so, unless he is dedicated, he's tempted to insure the bad risks, especially if his company has no control over the underwriting. A number of American insurance companies have experimented with preissue policies, but all but one have gone out of the business because it proved unprofitable. The sole exception has been Clem's Combined Group of Companies. He has attracted high-quality representatives who believe that honesty and integrity are the best policies.

He attributes his success with preissue policies to a number
of factors, but most of all to the way he trains his salesmen.
With his system of selling, his men can sell more plans in a
week than others can sell in months. They sell in small incre-
ments and concentrate on one policy at a time. The whole plan
is geared to repeated sales, which means that when the salesman calls back the following year, he sells additional incre-
ments. For this reason, he is as interested as the home office in
writing quality business. What's more, he saves the time that
other salesmen waste due to the additional call-backs that
home office underwriting and issuance of policies entail.

Of course, even great salesmen thrive on recognition and
appreciation. Clem Stone knows the name and record of every
salesman working for him. He is never too aloof to listen to
any one of his thousands of employees who may have a problem. Gradually, Clem Stone is turning over the reins of his
business interests to the strong management team that he has
developed. But he still travels extensively to the branches and
subsidiary headquarters of his companies, where he attends
training sessions, listens to problems, and even works in the
field, training new members of the sales force. His employees
regard him as a friend as well as a boss.

As he moves from one business achievement to the next,
Clem also continues to promulgate his ideas about success. At
first, he restricted his efforts to his own sales force and business
associates. Then, as he became convinced that he had discovered something from which everyone could profit, he spread
out into what is turning into a whole new career—helping
others.

Napoleon Hill influenced the direction that Clem's life took.
Until he read Hill's classic book, *Think and Grow Rich,* he had
never heard of Hill. For the first time he realized that others
besides himself had discovered the magic power of the mind.

Clem and Hill met in 1952, became close friends and combined their talents in several important projects. They were coauthors of a best-selling book, *Success Through a Positive Mental Attitude*. This led to the establishment of their PMA (Positive Mental Attitude) Science of Success course. This course, which consists of seventeen lessons, is taught all over the country to teen-agers, businessmen, teachers, and members of church groups.

Clem also started publishing and serving as editor-in-chief of *Success Unlimited*, an inspirational self-help monthly. He established the W. Clement and Jessie V. Stone Foundation to give financial and moral support to needy, deserving people.

In 1965, he purchased Hawthorn Books, Inc., publishers of nonfiction in the areas of history, biography, reference, religion, and art. Through Hawthorn, Clem is now developing a line of self-help books for use in classrooms from kindergarten through college, and is also publishing self-help books written for teachers.

In addition to these activities, he has become an authority on extrasensory perception and with Norma Lee Browning has written a book on the subject, *The Other Side of the Mind*. Among his close personal friends is Dr. Joseph Banks Rhine of Duke University, the "father" of ESP research in this country.

If I were to pinpoint his real interest in life today, I would say that Clem Stone has an unflagging ambition to motivate people to better their lives. He never delivers a talk, writes a letter, or carries on a conversation without this deep-seated interest in people showing through. He says that the fact that he has been a success shows that anybody can be a success. And he loves to help people find success.

He devotes as much of his personal time as he can to helping people. He especially loves to work with children. It is not unusual to find him at McCormick's Boys' Club in Chicago, teaching children how to read. And he spends a great deal of time with children at the Interlochen Arts Academy and National Music Camp in Michigan. At the recent inauguration of the camp's new president, when the board of directors were introduced one by one, Clem received an impressive and prolonged ovation, not just because he writes checks to help the children but because he has become involved in their lives.

But Clem realizes that he can be physically present in a limited number of places. And where he can't be in person, he tries to make his presence felt through financial help. "I can't be on a street corner with the Salvation Army, or with a missionary in Africa, or in an operating room by the side of a skilled surgeon. But I can be part of the work of all of these by contributing financially to their causes."

He has helped rehabilitate many criminals and dope addicts, particularly through Teen Challenge, which works with teen-aged delinquents. He has arranged for classes on motivational subjects to be given to inmates of jails and prisons. Since he is a firm believer in self-help books, he distributes free of charge hundreds of thousands of inspirational volumes to young people, his employees, company stockholders, schools, hospitals, veterans' organizations, and inmates of correctional institutions. In a single year, he has given away 100,000 hardcover books and a million paperbacks.

He especially enjoys helping talented people to realize their ambitions. He helped a prison inmate in Australia prepare for life outside the walls by purchasing two of his paintings. During a trip to Italy, he met Gualberto Rocchi, a Genoese sculptor. After seeing his work, including a bust of Richard Nixon now in the Senate gallery, Clem commissioned him to do busts of officials of his company and members of his family. Clem has sponsored several writers. Among them have been

John Walsh, author of *The Shroud* and of a biography of Francis Thompson, and James McGovern, who wrote *Crossbow and Overcast*.

He has backed several Broadway plays and was an investor in the national touring company of *Auntie Mame*. In addition, he has provided scholarships for dozens of gifted young musicians and is a major benefactor and trustee of the National Music Camp and Interlochen Arts Academy. He is board chairman of the American Foundation of Religion and Psychiatry, of which Dr. Norman Vincent Peale is president and cofounder, and he is a member of the National Executive Committee of the Boys' Clubs of America.

The average man might think that Clem Stone is spreading himself too thin with all these diverse business and philanthropic activities. But he has a theory about this, based on yet another of his wide-ranging interests. He has made a lifetime study of cycles, and today he is chairman of the board of the Foundation for the Study of Cycles. Clem believes that the study of cycles proves conclusively that growth of any kind—that of the economy, of a business, and even of a person—is destined to follow a pattern whereby a thing grows rapidly at first, then reaches maturity, levels off, and dies. The only catalyst that can change this inexorable cycle is the addition of new life, new blood, or new activity. For this reason, he believes that he continues to grow and will continue to do so only so long as he applies his imagination and diligence to substituting new growth trends for the old ones.

J. Harry Wood

In 1944, J. Harry Wood was vice-president of the general agency department for one of the great life insurance companies. He had one of the choice jobs in the industry. In April of that year, he walked into the office of the president and told him that he wished to resign. When the president recovered his composure, he said: "Until this morning, I had always believed you to be one of the smart young men in the insurance industry, destined to go far with our company. You have increased sales and reduced unit costs even more than I had hoped when I placed you in your present position. You have solved the main problems the company faced when you took over. All you would have to do in the future is keep your hands on the steering wheel and your foot on the accelerator. But now that I have just discovered you aren't the smart fellow I believed you to be, I accept your resignation as of today."

J. Harry did not resent the president's reaction. He expected and understood it. In the life insurance business at that time, executives simply did not switch from one company to another. Anyone who tried to was immediately suspect. Part of the reason for this feeling against change of jobs was due to the nature of the industry. Among insurance agents, where turnover represented a serious problem, men who switched companies seldom succeeded. All insurance executives knew this, and, without reasoning the matter through, they applied the generalization to executives as well as the field force.

When the news was out that he had resigned from one of the best jobs in the industry, J. Harry's friends wondered what had happened. Some guessed that he had been fired, some that he had lost his mind. One friend, after hearing some of the circumstances about the new position, commented sadly, "I am sorry to see anyone, especially you, do something merely for additional money."

Although the new position did pay more money, this friend misread Wood's motives. He failed to take into consideration the differences in motivations that make businessmen act as they do. Some work to make a good living. Some work to make a name for themselves in the company or in the industry. A few—a very few—are like J. Harry Wood; they work because they enjoy the thrill of accepting and coping with challenging assignments. Once they meet a challenge and solve it to their satisfaction, they become restless, and they will not be satisfied until a new array of challenges comes along to pique their interest.

Throughout his executive career, J. Harry Wood has changed jobs on an average of once every five years; three years was the shortest time, seven the longest. In each instance he left only after he had accomplished everything he had set out to do—and more. Always, the principals in the company that he was leaving were sorry to see him go. More than once, he gambled his entire career on a change fraught with dangers and uncertainties. The highlights of his career will help give the reader insights into the inner drives that have motivated this remarkable individual. From these, it will be easy to see that J. Harry has dared to be different by refusing to rest on his laurels.

When he was a boy in the Arkansas Ozarks, only two other people in his hometown attended college. J. Harry not only decided to go, but he was determined to earn most of his college expenses while he was still in high school. To this end, he held a number of jobs simultaneously. He worked in his father's store every Saturday. For a couple of years, he was the upstairs janitor of the high school. For a few weeks each year, he served as night hotel clerk and drove the taxi to meet the night trains. But he made most of his money in the fish-moss business. The way he got into this unusual occupation is indicative of later things in his career.

While on his first trip to Little Rock, he happened to be in the lobby of the Marion Hotel when one of the employees brought in some moss to put in the gold fish aquarium. J. Harry asked where he got the moss. "We buy it at a pet shop," he was told. J. Harry had a gold fish aquarium of his own. But it had never occurred to him that anyone would pay for moss. He raked his own out of the Spring River which flowed by his home town.

When he returned home, he wrote a dozen postmasters in nearby cities, asking for the names of pet shops. He received replies from every inquiry. He then wrote to the stores, offering to ship them fish moss at one cent per bunch of twelve strands. Orders came faster than he could fill them, so he raised the price to two cents and finally to three cents—at which point demand balanced with supply. During his junior year in high school, the cashier of the local bank told him that his income was among the first ten in the town.

In the fall of 1922, J. Harry Wood entered the University of Arkansas. He immediately started worrying about his grades. But at the end of the first term, he found that he stood ninth in the entire student body.

At the end of his second year in the university, he was offered a scholarship to Harvard. This was unusual because Harvard at that time accepted practically no transfers from other schools. For J. Harry, the decision was a difficult one. It meant that he had to leave a school where he was well-known and where his grades were high. Without quite realizing why, he accepted the scholarship. With hindsight, one can see now that his acceptance was a manifestation of his lifetime desire to meet new challenges.

He left the University of Arkansas campus in the spring of 1924. Little did he realize that his next visit would not be until January, 1964, when he returned to give the commencement address to the largest group of graduates up to that time.

Although Harvard allowed no more than a grade of C on courses taken in other universities, J. Harry graduated cum laude in 1926.

Many graduates at that time entered the professions or some field of finance. Few even considered the life insurance business, which was J. Harry's choice. When his father learned that he had joined an insurance company, he said, "The only people I have ever known who have gone into life insurance have been those who have failed in everything else. I don't see why you had to go to college if this was what you were going to do."

Although he was offered a position in a well-developed Group Sales Department of the largest of all insurance companies, he turned it down. Instead, he joined the John Hancock Life which was just entering the group field and had only two group cases in force. The department was not even fully staffed. But J. Harry reasoned that, if he could meet the challenge and survive the tougher assignment, his personal development and success would progress much faster.

One man in the department had had previous experience selling group life insurance. One day, this man had an appointment to go to Providence, Rhode Island, but was taken sick. Since the appointment was not considered to amount to anything, J. Harry was sent merely to keep it. This was the first day he ever made a sales call. Before he was through, he established a record which stood for a long time and has seldom been equaled since: he made sales to four different firms during the day, one to a general insurance agency which represented a life insurance company which also sold group insurance.

In each of the three years he stayed in the group department of John Hancock, J. Harry Wood led in number of sales by a very wide margin. Then, at the suggestion of the company officer who headed the ordinary sales department, he resigned to attend Columbia University where he took a master's degree in economics. He started his studies on October 1, and received his degree by February 1, or after four months of study.

He then returned to the company (his resignation was considered a leave of absence) in the ordinary sales department. He was assigned to the educational division, a new division not only for the company but for the industry. His job was to travel around the country training both new and experienced agents.

Within a short time, he was sent by the company to Ohio as manager of sales for a large agency, even though he had had no experience in hiring or supervising salesmen. In this spot, he worked with Ralph W. Hoyer, an outstanding general manager, one of the three men to whom he says he owes the most for his success (the others are Guy W. Cox, a president of John Hancock, and John Marshall Holcombe, Jr., former head of the Life Insurance Agency Management Association). While he was manager of sales, the agency moved from ninth to second place nationally.

Again, after three successful years, he was offered a job in the Life Insurance Agency Management Association. His job was divided into three distinct categories: (1) consultant to the sales departments of other life insurance companies; (2) instructor, later head, of schools for managers; and (3) writer of articles and books. In this period, he wrote one of the first complete training courses for new life insurance salesmen, *Successful Selling*.

After three successful years in this position, he received a call from the new president of John Hancock. This man offered him the job of head of John Hancock's ordinary sales department. Again, the challenge of the assignment was what attracted him. Company sales had been going downhill every year for the last ten years. His job was to reverse the trend, improve sales, and reduce unit costs at the same time.

This was by far the biggest job he had held. At that time, he was only thirty-one years old, one of the youngest men ever to be placed in such a position in any insurance company. In this industry, as in many others, men seldom reach this position before they are in their fifties.

With a handful of exceptions, the local managers within the company were all over age fifty, some over seventy as retirement plans had not yet become common. They were legally independent contractors; they had established habits or ways of doing, or not doing, things. Only four years before, the man now their leader had been sent into their agencies to help them in a minor part of their work. While they were universally friendly and sympathetic, they posed a solid front of resistance to changes that J. Harry Wood might have in mind.

His job was to get them to change. To reverse the trend of

declining sales, they would have to build their sales forces and to make them effective. This represented a considerable outlay of money for each of these managers, and it also meant that they would have to change their habits of work—which, as anyone who has ever supervised people knows, is the hardest of all to accomplish. The problem was to make these entrenched old-timers forget that they were dealing with a youngster they had known. Somehow, J. Harry had to convince them that they were dealing with someone who could really help them.

One of his old bosses said that Wood achieved what he wanted in a way which would seem very elementary today. But when he used the technique, it was the first time anyone had ever tried it. On large sheets, he made lists of all salesmen that each manager had hired during the past ten years, as well as those still with him who had been there ten years previously. Across the page was each man's production by years for as long as he lasted. Total sales and the number of men in the agency were shown for each year. J. Harry visited the managers in all sixty offices over the country. After a few minutes of pleasantries, he pulled out the particular manager's sheet, explained how it had been constructed, and how to read it. He than sat back and waited. It took the various managers from fifty minutes to three hours to digest what they were seeing. In almost every case, the shock to the manager was almost traumatic. From his own records, he was seeing himself as a failure. Until then, he had been assuming that he was successful in the eyes of the company simply because he still held his job, and had received no criticism.

Two managers reacted by flying into rages. A few became despondent. But most of them reacted as one man who said, "I didn't dream results were so terrible. I have never seen or heard of this kind of analysis before. I would like to do a good job. Moreover, I would like to do the job well enough in the next five years to make up for the last ten. Now, if you've been smart enough to make this analysis, I will assume you are smart enough to help me. What should I do?"

Whenever Wood received this reaction, he pulled out a tailor-made program that he had prepared. It showed exactly what to do, how, when, and by whom. Doubtless, no one can pinpoint and prove when scientific sales management was born. But there can be no doubt that this is one of the early instances when it was practiced.

The local agencies began to grow. Records began to be made. The home office organization began to be built.

In about seven years, the tough part of the job had been done. Sales were up and still going up. The number of branch offices and salesmen had increased dramatically. Unit costs had decreased year by year. The job was still a complicated one by any standards, but it now required less creative leadership and more management by exception. J. Harry had met the challenge. He had solved the difficult problems. Hardly conscious of it at the time, he began to feel the slowing down of the old drive.

Just at this very time, a man who was chief executive of three related insurance companies died suddenly. Boards of these three companies began to look for a successor. They settled on Wood. Stock, as well as a good salary, was involved. But the main, the chief, the all-important thing offered was a challenge of not only new problems but of a different kind of problem. He would now have to manage three companies simultaneously, two of them in lines of insurance in which he had not previously worked. He accepted the opportunity to manage the three companies which have since merged into the Paul Revere Life Insurance Company.

After almost six years here, he again realized that he had

accomplished what he set out to do. He needed new challenges. And this time, he was to accept a challenge that was radically different.

Back in the fall of 1929, when he was at the Columbia graduate school, the faculty members naturally assumed that he would be going into teaching. He had been offered several jobs as instructor in economics in well-known universities. These provided only a fleeting temptation at that time, but over the years, the idea of teaching continued to crop up.

His education had been in liberal arts schools, both undergraduate and graduate. But the schools of business were growing fast, and he was thrown in contact with them indirectly through hiring their graduates. He gradually formed the opinion that many of the graduates lacked a maturity about business. In discussing this thought with a couple of his friends who were deans of schools of business, he said: "Too many of these young graduates fail to see the effect of a new policy or change in their department on the entire company. Often, when they try to improve something in their own job or department, they unknowingly create problems for the rest of the company. They have studied accounting, principles of management, sales management, and all the other courses, but they fail to tie them together to make a related whole out of the parts."

The deans told him that many educators in the schools of business were conscious of this. Many thought that what was needed was a final course in business policy which would make use of the material in all the other courses previously studied. The Harvard Graduate School of Business and a few other universities had such a course. But the majority of schools did not.

The logical question was, "Why don't all schools of business have such a course?" The deans gave several reasons. One was lack of teachers who would attempt it. Teaching such a course would take not only a rounded background in business and economics but also experience in making high-level business decisions. One of the deans said, "Why don't you tackle it?"

J. Harry replied that he had never studied in a school of business, nor did he have a working knowledge of all the courses. "Oh, yes, you have," they said and proceeded to explain why they believed him to have knowledge of most of the courses. "At your present age," they said, "you would be welcome at any one of a dozen schools right now."

The wheels began to turn in Wood's mind. He was the right age. He was financially able to take such a job. The challenge had begun to fade in his present work. The dean of the School of Business at Washington University, St. Louis, said, "Come with us as Professor of Business Management and teach this course." So, he did, beginning with the second semester in February, 1950.

J. Harry Wood's acceptance of this position took remarkable courage. Here he was, a young businessman, outstanding in his industry, who voluntarily took on a teaching assignment when he had never taught, and never attended a school of business, and had never studied any of the formal courses to which his students would already have been exposed. Besides, he had to start teaching within two weeks after acceptance, and he had to construct the course from scratch because it had never been offered before.

His approach was as simple as it was ingenious. While many schools had had successful businessmen present a lecture or two to some classes or the student body, none had used them as effectively as J. Harry Wood. As part of his new course, he built his policy studies around a company. Each week, the company sent out heads of its departments to explain and discuss with the class the policies of their departments and how these policies meshed in with over-all company policy. In the final week, the president led the discussion and showed how all the elements tied together.

For two years in succession, the president of Cluett, Peabody volunteered for his company to make this contribution. Ralston Purina, the largest company in St. Louis, cooperated for another two successive years, and Sears Roebuck for one year.

The reactions of participating executives were interesting. The vice-presidents and other department heads always said two things: "Getting ready for the three hours (one and one-half hours of lecture, one and one-half hours of answering questions) forced us to organize and rethink about our own policies, which we had not done for some time before." And the second thing they said was, "We'd give anything to be able to sit in on the lectures and discussions led by the other officers of our company because we would learn more about the company than anyone, except the president, now knows."

The president of Ralston Purina made an interesting comment: "If you are talking with any company about participating and they hesitate, have them call me. Ralston Purina entered this primarily to make a contribution to a university located in our own community and, hopefully, to help blaze a new path in schools of business. But as it happens, we have gotten more than we have given. It has educated us all as we have prepared the material. I was amazed at how many conflicting policies of which I was not aware had developed within the company because of the passage of time or the idiosyncrasies of individuals."

While at Washington University, Wood took a leave of absence for a year to help a life insurance company that had a problem. In that time, he eliminated sizable annual losses in one of the departments, and also helped bring about a merger with another company with common ownership. This was a consultant's job, but he assumed the title of president in order to do the job quickly and effectively.

At approximately the same time he had accepted the teaching job at Washington University, he was asked to be editor of *The CLU Journal,* a professional magazine publishing original articles in the fields of economics, estate planning, investments, marketing, research, taxation, and all phases of life insurance operations. He accepted this position and held it for eight years.

In his capacity as editor of *The CLU Journal,* he had to decide on the topics he wanted written about, find authorities who were also able to write, and then get them to do the work for free. To do this, he had to know enough, or be able to find out enough, not only to catch errors but also, in many cases, to make the preliminary outlines for the articles.

During this period, he published a number of articles on inflation and life insurance in both Germany and Japan. Already interested in South America, he took a sabbatical from Washington University and spent the time in the various South American countries studying the cause and effects of inflation and what was being done about it.

While in South America, he learned of the high regard that many there held for the University of Miami. When the dean of the School of Business of the University of Miami asked him to be a Professor of Finance, he accepted.

Once he became proficient in teaching in his new field of endeavor, he was open to new challenges. One of his best friends was chairman of the board of the Life Insurance Agency Management Association. This gentleman got in touch with Wood to tell him that the managing director of LIAMA had just left. "We, the board, want you to take it. You owe it to the industry. We have some problems which we think you can help solve. The job itself straddles the academic and business worlds."

He took it. In effect, three threads of his life came together at this time: (1) a lifetime of study and practice of management which had led to the conclusion that the principles are substantially the same in all businesses and in all countries, (2) a knowledge of economic history, and (3) the knowledge of the effect of lack of capital in South America.

So in 1960, at the annual meeting of the Life Insurance Agency Management Association, he proposed the carrying of management principles and know-how to other countries through the medium of the LIAMA's schools of management. The association's literature on management had long been sent to these member countries, but this wasn't enough. In his talk, he said:

Why this interest on our part? Governments cannot do some things as well as private industry. That is a beautiful thought, but it is also stupid to even express it unless private industry is willing to do something. So the first reason for our interest is to implement thoughts and slogans to which only lip service has been given by so many in various industries in the past. In short, we propose that life insurance be a leader.

In a broader sense, the institution of life insurance may be far more important, more essential to the free world, than we have believed. Let me remind you that democracy is impossible without a middle class. Try to find an exception; it is doubtful if you can.

Life insurance is necessary for the existence of a middle class. An industrial commercial society is a requirement for a middle class. A country has this kind of society when it has factories, dams, banks, commerce.

In many countries of the world, the institution of life insurance can be of great help in the collection and loaning out of the savings of the people.

But the growth of life insurance depends upon the

development of successful sales outlets. That is where LIAMA comes in.

Without a middle class, you have a dictatorship, either of the right or of the left. Governments, realizing this, attempt to move time ahead by gifts, loans, Point Four programs. But sometime this, too, must end. When it does, will there be something to take its place—savings institutions, including life insurance?

And life insurance is necessary for another reason: to preserve the middle class. For otherwise, on the death of the breadwinner the children go to work instead of to school; too often they would slide back, down from the middle class.

Through Wood's pioneering efforts, Life Insurance Agency Management schools have been set up in twelve foreign countries. The first of two was established in Japan in 1960. Since then, two have been set up in South Wales, two in England, two in France, two in South Africa, one in Venezuela, and one in Australia.

The position of managing director of the Life Insurance Agency Management Association is such that the one occupying it is, or becomes, widely known in the industry. Presidential offers came often. J. Harry politely shunted these aside until he was approached to head up the 107-year-old Home Life Insurance Company of New York. He says that he accepted partly for sentimental reasons (he had been a consultant to it twenty-five years previously), partly because of admiration for its officers and members of the Board of Directors, partly because it was old and substantial, partly because it made use of a professional type of selling known as planned estates, but mostly because of its challenge. Sales had remained on a plateau for several years; its share of the national market had been declining, and costs were relatively high.

Needless to say, this chapter of his life would not be included if the results had not been dramatic—and they have been! The size of the company during the seven years he has been there, measured by millions in force, has almost doubled. Annual sales have more than doubled, and costs to policyholders are now extremely low—among the very best, as Wood's competitors well know.

J. Harry states with sincerity and conviction that these results have come about because of the abilities of the individuals in the company and their team work. And, of course, this is true. No football team ever gets results unless the individual players have ability and unless they play as a team. But for them to be a winning team, there has to be a great coach.

There are many success stories in American business. Perhaps, J. Harry Wood's has happened simply because he has had to be different to remain true to his nature. He thrives on challenge. Each successive challenge he has faced has renewed him, so that he's always like a young knight going forth in quest for adventure. He has such zest for life that some of it rubs off on everyone with whom he comes in contact.

Harry R. White

When we told Harry White that we wanted to include him in this book, his reaction was "Why me? I'm the most un-different guy I know of. Same job for almost thirty-five years!"

But Harry underestimates his contribution to the marketing and sales field. He had the courage to remake a lackluster, inbred sales-executives club, consisting of seventy-five members, into one of the most exciting and influential organizations on the current business scene. When his bosses said that it couldn't be done, Harry, through persistence, inventiveness, and sheer cussedness, proved that it could.

His first day on the job as executive secretary of the newly formed Sales Executives Club of New York set the stage for the problems he was to face. The president of the club greeted him with these words: "This is a small organization. We want to keep it that way. So, consider this as a steppingstone because you'll never make more than twenty-five dollars a week on this job."

That was thirty-four years ago. Looking back, Harry thinks that the president's myopic statement constituted the challenge that, over the years, kept him turning down better paying offers, even when his chances of changing the thinking of his board of directors looked pretty bleak.

Originally, he had taken the job as a stopgap measure until

he could get into newspaper work. He had just graduated from Columbia University School of Journalism, and it was the depths of the depression. Thousands of experienced newspapermen were looking for work.

One day he received a letter from Columbia's placement office. It told about a business club that had just been formed. The club needed a secretary who could write its bulletins, mimeograph them, mail them out, and handle all of the organization's other business besides. The pay was twenty dollars a week—a relatively good starting salary in those days. This wasn't a newspaper job. But it was a job. And Harry needed it.

He applied and discovered that all seventy-six members of the graduating class in journalism had been notified of the opportunity. Most of them were as eager as Harry to land the job. The member of the club's board of directors who was assigned to do the screening was swamped with applications. In desperation, he decided to interview only the top 5 percent of the graduating class.

As an average student, Harry knew he didn't stand much of a chance against such formidable odds. He would have to do something radically different to get the favorable consideration of the selection committee.

He obtained a list of the directors of the club and interviewed as many as he could reach. He visited a newspaper morgue and read everything he could find about the formation of the new club. Then he made a list of the problems faced by the fledgling organization. After each problem he wrote his proposed solution, based on information he had gleaned from his interviews. Then he bought a pack of penny postcards (yes, they were a penny in those days!). Every day he mailed one of the cards to the chairman of the selection committee. On each card was a problem, plus Harry's proposed solution.

After three weeks of this, he received a phone call informing him that he was the winner. Later he was told that the committee had made up its mind to hire him after the first week of the postcard barrage. But they were intrigued by the ingenuity of the approach—and they didn't want to stop the flow of ideas and solutions. (Being different sometimes has its penalties, even if it does get results!)

Few people have started a job under more discouraging circumstances. A less determined man would have quit at the end of the first week. Harry's first visitors were bill collectors for printing firms, the hotel, an office-furniture dealer, three stationery stores, and other suppliers.

Members who had dropped into the club office had run up an astronomical phone bill which hadn't been paid. So the phone company had discontinued service. Harry persuaded the company to install a pay phone behind his desk. Every time he wanted to make a call, he had to put a nickel in the slot. A great many people got the impression that the secretary of the Sales Executives Club of New York, Inc., worked out of a phone booth.

These were problems he hadn't anticipated in his postcard campaign. There were plenty more to come. But the immediate problem was to raise some money quickly to hold off the sheriff.

Harry had started the use of door prizes at the weekly luncheon meetings to motivate those present to fill out and hand in their attendance cards. Since the cards were used in the drawing, anyone who didn't hand in his card was out of the drawing. Harry was struck by two phenomena: the willingness of members to donate merchandise as prizes in return for a plug from the platform; and the eagerness with which even top executives strive to win a prize—regardless of value. As a matter of fact, Harry observed that the higher the man is on the economic scale, the more eager he seems to be to get something for nothing.

With Christmas coming on, Harry decided to put on a party featuring prize giveaways. A now-extinct nightclub on 57th Street, with the unlikely name of Le Boeuf Sur le Toit, took a chance on his little group with the bad credit rating. Nearly every member of the club donated at least one prize. Free entertainment was lined up by Count Gosta Morner, a genuine Swedish nobleman who was then a talent agent. (The Count discovered such stars as Bob "Bazooka" Burns and Jan Peerce.)

The party was a success. The nightclub was packed. With the surplus realized from the sale of tickets, Harry was able to pay off the club's debts.

Every year this popular Christmas Party has grown in size and elaborateness. It is now the largest businessmen's Christmas gathering in the world. In 1967, 4,400 members and their guests packed two large ballrooms of the New York Hilton Hotel. By alternating the acts, Harry had a stage show running simultaneously in each ballroom. The prize list, with a total value of at least half a million dollars, included four completely equipped automobiles and a roundtrip for two to Hong Kong, with hotel accommodations. Surplus from these giant parties goes toward support of the club's selling-as-a career activities with high schools and colleges, as well as other public service projects.

As he became more deeply involved in the work, Harry grew more and more fascinated by it. Organizing the weekly luncheons brought him into contact with interesting bigwigs in selling, general business management, government, and the arts. He had an opportunity to put his training in journalism to good advantage in writing the weekly club bulletin and various promotion pieces.

But his real fascination was centered on the leaders of the selling profession. They seemed almost depression-proof. While others were pinching pennies and singing the blues, sales managers were optimistic and prosperous. Business needed them now as never before. They were important men in their companies. With a few exceptions, they were broad-minded and willing to try almost anything new.

Salesmanship fascinated the new club manager. Like many who are not connected with the profession—or art, as many insist—he had previously identified it with the foot-in-the-door boys and peripatetic wooers of farmers' daughters. But no business could get along without them for long. They kept the free enterprise system running. Their persuasion had built whole industries. Even top executives felt flattered to be called master salesmen.

But Harry was surprised by the welter of theories about how to sell and the disorganized state of the profession. Every other sales manager or salesman seemed to have the true formula for selling success which he would someday expose to the waiting world in the form of a book. Marketing as we know it today was practically nonexistent. The factory ran the show. The sales department was handed the product and told to go out and sell it. Market research was just beginning to gain some acceptance, but there was a tendency to scoff at it as "long-hair stuff."

Perhaps, thought Harry, the Sales Executives Club of New York could do something to make selling more professional. But he knew that he couldn't accomplish much with only seventy-five members. Growth was imperative.

It is hard to believe today that he could have encountered resistance to increasing the size of the club. But if one reflects on it, the situation becomes understandable. In a small club, everyone knows everyone else. Everybody serves on a committee. The chances of serving on the board of directors are good. So are the chances of getting to be president. These are all advantages that a small organization has over a large one, and they appeal to men who enjoy personal contact and self-expression. But they are not conducive to growth and progress.

Harry knew what had to be done, but he faced two handicaps: he was inexperienced, and he looked it. Gangling and shy, with a shock of blond hair—since copiously depleted—he looked like a schoolboy. In meetings of the board of directors, he was ordered to take notes and speak only when spoken to. How could a kid like that hope to change basic policy? But he remembered something told to him by his father, Frank White, the great organist who worked with many theater and symphony orchestras: "Son, when you're with a bunch of prima donnas and can't make yourself heard, sell a strong man in the group on your ideas and get him to go to bat for you."

Harry found a strong man in the person of the chairman of the membership committee, James M. Thornton, sales manager for a coffee company. A diminutive, cigar-chewing North Carolinian, Jim was an irresistible salesman, with a Fred Allen twang, a prodigious memory, and a leechlike persistence when he decided something ought to be done. His favorite hobby was getting members for the club. He personally had brought in three quarters of those then registered.

Harry found Thornton a willing listener to his ideas for expansion. Thornton agreed to do a selling job on the directors. But he got voted down. "You'll ruin the club if it goes over a hundred members," he was told.

Harry again went into a huddle with Thornton. They discussed the strategy, and in the end Thornton again proved his mettle by agreeing to a revolutionary approach. He decided to throw out the no-progress clique at the next election.

A battle royal, unique in the annals of club work, ensued.

John A. Zellers, vice-president of Remington Rand, Inc., agreed to run as a write-in candidate in opposition to the regularly nominated administration candidate. A war chest was raised for mailings, proxies, campaign banners, buttons, and pencils. Thornton called every member of the club by phone and urged a write-in vote for Zellers. The New York press became intrigued with the battle and reported it in depth. Sales executives, reading and hearing about this live-wire organization, wanted to join. The whole club was revitalized by a campaign which many had predicted would cause its dissolution in a welter of dissension and bad feeling.

John Zellers won. The sky was now the official limit. Harry had won the first important step in his campaign to prove that the Sales Executives Club was not destined to be just a small, sociable nonentity. But there was another battle ahead.

It's one thing to want growth. It's another thing to achieve it. Harry's own personal efforts to sell new members had convinced him that this was a full-time job for somebody. Nearly everything worthwhile in this world has to be sold. Why not find a salesman to sell memberships in the club? This seemed a natural development for an organization of sales executives.

Because of the time he had spent on the election campaign, Jim Thornton had lost his job at the coffee company. Harry proposed to the directors that the club hire Thornton to sell memberships on a commission basis.

Well, these progressive, growth-conscious, sales-minded executives were shocked to the depths of their BVDs. The idea of hiring a man to sell anything as universally desirable as a membership in the Sales Executives Club seemed scandalous to them. "What," one of them asked, "would people say if it leaked out that we had to hire a salesman to lure people into our club?"

Harry went to work on the president and a few other key

executives like Fen K. Doscher, then district sales manager
for Lily-Tulip Cup Corp. Harry argued that the Sales Executives Club is an organization devoted to the concept of salesmanship as the prime mover of the economy. He pointed out
that the club had a sales problem that could be solved only by
continuous, well-motivated salesmanship.

He finally received an official but cautious go-ahead from
the directors. They would try it for one month. If even one
complaint about it was registered, personal solicitation would
be discontinued immediately. The situation was like sitting on
a bomb—waiting for a complaint and, at the same time, des-
perately covering every possible source of complaint to keep
one from developing.

New members were rolling in at the rate of one a day. All
of them were either leaders of the selling profession or presidents of companies interested in giving their personal support
to the selling function. Harry and Jim were running no risk of
having someone charge that paid solicitation was watering
down the caliber of the membership.

As the club rapidly grew, full-time, paid solicitation became
an accepted fact of life. Other clubs and associations, observing
the success of the Sales Executives Club, tried the same
formula. Readers would be shocked by the names of some of
the distinguished and exclusive clubs that tried to hire Jim
Thornton away from the Sales Executives Club. In those days
of the depression, practically all clubs were hurting due to the
general lack of money and members.

After Thornton gave up the job because of ill health, Harry
conceived the idea of having retired sales executives carry on
the job of selling memberships. He believes that men who
have been active in the club can handle such a delicate selling
job most effectively. They enjoy standing in the club and can
project a good personal image to a prospect for membership.

And since money is not an urgent matter with them, they concentrate on quality and take special pride in the job they are doing. Harry believes in treating these men not as employees but as honored members, which they are.

For the past five years, the club's director of membership has been a popular past-president, Joseph L. Wood, retired treasurer of Johns-Manville Corp. A rare combination of natural-born salesman and financial man, Joe is setting new records for membership growth. It is this sort of dedicated person that Harry continually looks for to help him achieve his objectives for the club.

As another example, about ten years ago a man came to him for advice in getting a job. This person had been with an association and wanted to continue in association work. His name was Henry K. Astwood. Harry White was intrigued with this man's emphasis on getting a challenging assignment, with remuneration and security secondary considerations. He was just the kind of man that Harry liked to work with. But he had no budget to hire him.

At the time, Harry had just started a weekly magazine for the club, with advertising defraying part of the cost of production. He asked Astwood if he would be interested in trying his hand at selling the ads on a commission basis until a broader opportunity came up. Astwood agreed, although he had never sold an ad before in his life.

Harry gave him a desk and a phone. Within a month, Hank Astwood had sold several thousand dollars' worth of ads, putting the magazine on an almost-break-even basis.

Hank also showed an interest in helping sales executives and salesmen get jobs. It wasn't long before he was handling this part of the club's service as a sideline. His natural skill at handling these problems created more and more demands on his time. And at the same time, companies in need of selling talent were knocking at the club's door in ever-increasing numbers. Here was a great need, and an opportunity for a full-time service. But such a service, properly organized, would cost a good deal more money than the club's budget could afford.

Harry asked Hank if he would be willing to take another big gamble. The club would set up a full-scale clearinghouse for sales and marketing talent, financed by an annual contribution from each company that made regular use of the services. There would be no fees charged to individuals.

This was the beginning of the Sales Manpower Foundation. It met with vociferous opposition from professional personnel counselors, many of whom were members of the club. They felt that a nonprofit organization that they supported was horning in on the profit sector and posing the threat of competition. Harry solved that one with a two-step formula. He convinced the objectors that the Foundation files would be a source of help to every cooperating personnel consulting organization. And he put these personnel counselors on the committee supervising the operation. Many became charter members of the Foundation, paying $250 each per year.

Today, after six years of operation under Hank Astwood's direction, the Sales Manpower Foundation is known and respected throughout the nation. It has thousands of résumés. and job specifications in its well-kept files. It conducts continuous research on sales compensation and selling costs, industry by industry. And it supervises the famous Man Marketing Clinic, an advisory group that has met every Tuesday evening under club auspices for the past thirty-three years, advising people on the best ways to market their talents and prepare job résumés.

One unusual aspect of the Foundation is that it pays its own way, and has from the start. So the Sales Executives Club has acquired a valuable and unique service without adding to its expense budget. This is important in a nonprofit organization that depends largely on membership dues. There is never enough money to pay for all the things you want to do or all the things you need. So you have to devise ingenious methods to get others to put up the money or to volunteer their services.

Take the problem of speakers. Many speakers who are in demand expect to get honorariums, or at least their expenses. This was a problem especially in the early days of the Sales Executives Club, when the club was unable to boast a sizable membership—much less pay fees or expenses. How could a small, impoverished organization get some of the nation's most important personalities to address its weekly luncheons? Harry solved this by creating awards for the speakers he wanted.

This first occurred to him when he was trying to get an acceptance from one of the greatest salesmen and business tycoons of modern times, Charles M. Schwab. He had been turned down repeatedly by the great man. When Mr. Schwab was reported to be ailing and under a doctor's care, it looked as though that was the end of it. But Harry thought he'd try one more time. And this time he'd put some special bait on the hook. He invited Mr. Schwab to be the first recipient of the Distinguished Salesman Award—an honor he dreamed up on the spur of the moment.

By return mail, he received an invitation to visit Mr. Schwab at his mansion on Riverside Drive to discuss the matter. With a belly full of butterflies, Harry journeyed to the fabled address on the Hudson River. As he entered, he found Mr. Schwab enjoying an organ concert in the great hall. It was an honest-to-God pipe organ—not one of the new electronic gadgets.

After the concert, Mr. Schwab invited Harry into his study. Fixing him with piercing blue eyes, the great steelmaster said:

"Young man, what is this Distinguished Salesman Award? Who created it? Why are you offering it to me?"

Harry knew it would be useless to fib to this man. "Well, sir," stammered Harry, "I made up the award myself. We've wanted to honor you for a long time, but you've turned me down five times. I thought I'd try once more. I needed a reason I hadn't offered you before. I thought of an award. And that's it." Harry prepared to reach for his hat.

A twinkle lit up the blue eyes. Chuckling, Mr. Schwab said: "My doctor tells me I'm a sick man. He refuses to allow me to attend any more meetings or make any more speeches. But I like that award, and I want it. I've always admired salesmen and salesmanship. It may shorten my life. But I'll be there to get it. And I'll do the best I can with a speech."

And he did. His last public appearance was the Sales Executives Club meeting on April 27, 1939. Scores of presidents and board chairmen were in the audience to honor the legendary man, including the president of every major steel company. A doctor at his side, Mr. Schwab rose and, with tears in his eyes, delivered a moving tribute to the selling profession.

Reported by the daily and business press in detail, this meeting gave the Sales Executives Club a tremendous boost. Other eminent personalities were attracted by the award, and the club's weekly luncheons became one of the most sought-after forums in the United States.

Shortly after World War II, the award became known as the Applause Award. Seeking something more dramatic and distinctive than a silver plaque, Harry asked the French sculptor, Robert Bros, to design something that would symbolize the applause of the audience. Bros created a remarkably lifelike carving of hands in the typical posture of enthusiastic applause. Fashioned of mahogany and lignum vitae, the sculpture is a work of art and a conversation piece wherever it is displayed.

The Applause Award is given once a year to some outstanding business or government leader selected by the club's directors "for outstanding salesmanship and public service." Among the recipients have been Thomas J. Watson (both Senior and Junior), Dwight D. Eisenhower, David Sarnoff, Henry Ford II, Alfred P. Sloan, Jr., George Romney, James A. Farley, Eleanor Roosevelt, Richard M. Nixon, Nelson Rockefeller, and Charles Percy.

In another instance, Harry achieved a dramatic and effective solution to a problem by using a different approach. For many years the selling profession has been worried about its image. Too many young people, parents, and educators have had a mental picture of the salesman as the fellow who gets the door slammed in his face. Books, plays, movies, and television dramas like *Death of a Salesman* have contributed to the false notions of what the great majority of salesmen do and the way they live. With business expanding every year and young people reluctant to go into selling, American industry has reached what *Time* magazine calls the "marketing manpower crisis."

Ever since its founding, the Sales Executives Club has been concerned with the problem and has been a leader in developing ways to solve it. It has sparked other business and trade associations to undertake similar programs to help change the public's attitude toward business generally and selling specifically. But the problem has been to get the message to the general public. Most of the efforts have wound up with businessmen speaking to themselves or to relatively small groups of the public. Harry felt that a dramatic effort to reach a sizable segment of the thinking public was needed.

Here again was the problem of money. To reach people by the millions requires a sizable hunk of cash—more than the average nonprofit organization can afford. Harry decided that a special section in a Sunday edition of *The New York Times* would convey a prestige picture of selling to the national circulation of 1.65 million. Perhaps a large part of the cost could be defrayed by advertisements from companies interested in recruiting sales talent. This category includes most of the major firms in America.

When Harry proposed the project to the club's directors, they were intrigued with the idea. But most of them thought he could never swing it. They figured that, if the club were to come near breaking even, it would have to charge $6,200 per page to advertisers, considerably more than the page rate then for *The New York Times Magazine.*

But Harry had done his homework before the meeting. He had already sent letters to the presidents of twelve companies with modern, aggressive sales organizations and sales recruitment budgets. He presented the special section as a medium for recruitment rather than advertising. He pointed out that, if each participant got just one good salesman as a result, his investment would be well worthwhile. As an added inducement, Harry promised each prospective advertiser that only one firm in an industry would be accepted for the issue. This would give each advertiser the maximum return for his participation.

Of the twelve approached, five agreed to take full pages. Harry considered this a pretty good rate of return. So did the club directors. They authorized him to go ahead with the project, even if it didn't break even. They felt that the added publicity and prestige produced by such a publication would have a beneficial effect on every club activity from luncheon attendance to new memberships.

So Harry mailed more of his letters and received more pledges of support in return. His able administrative assistant, Ed Flanagan—a man with ten years' selling experience

—followed up the pledges and worked with the advertising agencies to produce effective recruitment copy. A professional writer with a solid sales background, Jack Tarrant, was retained to edit and lay out the issue. This assignment was not easy, for the objective was to appeal to four major groups of readers: high school and college students, their teachers and advisers, sales and marketing executives, and the general public.

And so, on November 19, 1967, appeared the biggest single effort up to that time to carry the story of selling and business careers to a large segment of the American public. The reaction surprised even the most optimistic supporters of the project. The club office and advertisers were flooded with inquiries. Orders came in for well over half a million additional copies. It is estimated that, with the pass-on readership, over 5 million people have been exposed to the special section. A by-product of the publication was the acquisition of more than three hundred new members in the Sales Executives Club.

Today, the Sales Executives Club of New York with 3,450 members stands as a living tribute to Harry White's determination and foresight. He has dared to be different by thinking for himself. He has had the ingenuity to take different approaches to problems and to put new twists on old routines. In the process, he has managed to outsell the master salesmen for whom he has always worked.

John Bodette

John Bodette dares to be different in a way that should give pause to every ambitious business-man: He has the courage to be a leader. And in a sense, every business leader worthy of the name charts a dangerous course. Once he starts playing it safe, he's a has-been. But always he must face the other possibility: one serious miscalculation, and he's out of a job.

In 1956, John was asked to head up the Florists' Trans-world Delivery Association. For some time, the association had been drifting along without making any significant prog-ress. Sales had leveled off, and the membership was, at best, lackadaisical about association activities. The board of direc-tors of the association decided that the only way to get things moving was to put a strong leader at the helm. Although John had no previous association experience, the board, after a thor-ough investigation of his successes in other fields, handpicked him for the job.

From the point of view of John's career, the situation was fraught with dangers. Members were agitating for action in half a dozen conflicting directions. Like most shopkeepers, these people were individualists. John knew from the beginning that he would be in for a hard time trying to get them pulling together. And, if he failed, the job as well as some of his carefully built reputation as a man who gets things done would go up in smoke.

His first major test as a leader turned up almost immediately, for with the job he inherited a rather messy internal conflict. He discovered that the association's sales and advertising committee was engaged in a knock-down-drag-out fight with its advertising agency. The situation had reached the point where neither side was willing to give an inch. The agency insisted that its advertising strategy was on the right track and that it should be kept unchanged. Most of the committee members were in favor of dropping the agency and finding one with a more flexible attitude.

After listening to both sides, John decided that the agency was right. But, as any good executive must do, he weighed his chances of getting his way if he threw his full support behind the agency's program. The members of the sales and advertising committee were among the most influential members of the association, including several members of the board of directors. They had, in effect, just hired him, and he knew that he would be taking a chance if he started bucking the power structure before he had time to accomplish something constructive.

On the other hand, he realized that he had two things going for him. The members would expect him to make some ripples if he were really going to give direction to the association. Further, he had already sensed from conversations he had had with many of the florists that these people could take criticism if it were constructive and valid. And when businessmen will accept rather strong criticism of their way of conducting their business affairs, and, in effect, give you a mandate to help them, you have at least a fighting chance when you choose a course of action that they may not favor.

John decided to take the chance, and he backed the agency.

Subsequent results proved that he was right. Thus, he started his career with the association by opposing some of the very men who hired him. But I should point out here that success was not due to his pursuing a hardheaded course without weighing the odds inherent in the situation.

A businessman learns to do this from experience. In John's case, he learned this on one of his first executive assignments in a publishing firm. He had been given the task of putting together an advertising and promotion campaign. The first thing he did was hire a new advertising agency. Only then did he discover that the former agency had been handpicked by the board chairman. John had neglected to check all bases before making a major change—to find out the important aspects of the situation, the ones that are readily evident and the personal relationships that you have to dig to uncover. Fortunately, he came out of this particular situation with only a few lumps to show for his carelessness. And he learned a valuable lesson that he has never forgotten.

When he joined Florists' Transworld Delivery, the association was clearing about 6.5 million orders totaling $48 million. He told the board of directors that the association could clear $100 million in the sixties. And, until that objective was achieved on December 1, 1966, he took his share of chiding for setting such a lofty goal. In effect, with less than four months of exposure to the flower industry, he had settled on pursuing a sales goal that seemed almost impossible—a 100 percent increase in sales amounting to $52 million.

While this goal seemed almost reckless to casual observers, John Bodette was confident that his background enabled him to set it because he was familiar with what it takes to accomplish sales advances. As a book publishing sales manager (with a firm other than the one already mentioned), he had been involved in all of the intricacies of subscription selling.

For years, he had successfully coped with quotas for various types of selling, time schedules, promotion campaigns, forecasting for inflationary and purchase-pattern changes, and other sales goal factors.

And he had some inside knowledge going for him about markets. He knew that consumers at that time were moving into a period in which they were going to start buying in a big way the so-called nicer things of life—products and services that feed the soul instead of just lining the belly and outfitting the home. Flowers for self-consumption and gifts were, he was sure, among the items that were going to enjoy a marked sales upswing.

However, he had obstacles to face. As any salesman knows, it's almost impossible to motivate a dealer effectively without a club of some kind—incentive plans, special discounts, quotas, contests, loss of franchise, and the like. None of these was available to Bodette. FTD florists are independent businessmen and women, and flowers-by-wire orders then represented only 15 percent of the volume of an average member florist.

One of John's early suggestions, made off the top of his head at a general meeting, was to standardize a floral arrangement and build a special cornucopia of flowers for a Thanksgiving Day promotion. This thought was so abhorrent to the Sales and Advertising Committee that John was violently opposed. He can still remember the late Joe Johnston, a respected multiple-shop owner in Pennsylvania, screaming objections at the top of his lungs. And, Larry Stapleton, the account executive at Grant Advertising, now staff vice-president—advertising and sales promotion—for TWA, took John aside for some friendly advice about avoiding the word "standardized" when floral artists were present.

Once again, experience played a part in his making an unconventional suggestion. He was talking about an entirely *new* product for the association. He knew what a new item can do to sales because he had once before successfully developed and promoted something that really took off. At the time, he was working for the Military Service Company, a southern firm specializing in the military market. Among the things that MSC produced were Field Manuals, or "FM's" as servicemen commonly know them. It struck John that, while there were FM's for just about any military activity, weapon or technique, there was no general reference and study work and no way for the enlisted man to update his professional library to keep pace with fast-moving changes.

With the help of a retired Army colonel, he developed a book produced in loose-leaf form so new information pages could be added easily. The publication, called the Army Notebook (later there was an Air Force Notebook), was pocket-size and equipped with dividers to help organize the material. While poles apart in conception, the notebook and John's standardized floral arrangement had a lot in common, although his floral suggestion seemed doomed to die.

However, John Bodette is a determined man, and the more he thought about the value of standardizing floral arrangements sold to consumers who seldom have a chance to see what they buy, the more attractive the idea became. He therefore decided to sell his idea in a roundabout way. At a board of directors meeting, he obtained permission to hire Dr. Ernest Dichter's Institute for Motivational Research to execute an in-depth study of public attitudes toward florists and floral purchases. When the questions for the survey were being prepared, John proposed that a number of questions probe consumer attitudes toward the service. One inquiry was directed to nonusers of the service. The great majority of nonusers indicated that they were skeptical of the service. They said that they had no guarantee what would be delivered, often to locations thousands of miles away from the place where they might place an order.

The $25,000 spent on that survey was returned to FTD florists a hundred times over. For John Bodette was now able, on the basis of the survey findings, to convince the association that it publish an annual catalog of "standardized" arrangements that could be ordered in any FTD shop, and delivered by any other FTD shop essentially as shown. This was a tough sell to the FTD board of directors, but John was helped by a new marketing committee whose members were willing to back his proposal in the face of some violent opposition.

Today, the association annually prints over 12 million FTD Selection Guides. The appearance of these guides each fall is to the floral industry what the annual new model introduction is to the auto industry—a pacesetter for style and design, a boon to increased sales. Without question, this innovation stands as the biggest single factor in FTD's achieving the $100 million goal in the mid-sixties.

Not content with the domestic success, Bodette powered this "standardized" concept through his international affiliate, Interflora. And, today, you can visit any of the 27,000 FTD-Interflora shops in over ninety countries, pick up a catalog, and send a floral arrangement anywhere in the world. In Stockholm, for example, you can select from a full-color photograph a floral arrangement to be delivered in Australia, and you can be assured that what you are viewing will be delivered as shown.

The development of this unique merchandising tool evolved from a series of decisions that John Bodette made. But, the success and ultimate wisdom of those decisions only came about because his staff came up with an effective mix—awareness of the strengths and weaknesses of the people who would be asked to use the tool, a knowledge of consumer attitudes obtained by using the most sophisticated research methods, a sense of timing to utilize a favorable committee makeup, and careful use of financial resources to produce a beautiful, full-color catalog that florists could not ignore.

John admits that at times he feels somewhat akin to Captain Bill Carpenter, Army's lonely end and Vietnam hero who called for a napalm attack on his own position during the battle of Toumorong. General William C. Westmoreland said at the Silver Star presentation, "You have shown courage, stamina, *and just plain* guts." Businessmen's only reward from a frequent application of these ingredients to a daring course of action is the agonizing and then exhilarating experience of watching the upward curve of a sales chart, or the satisfaction of a beautiful profit and loss statement.

In thinking about John's success, we can't help thinking also about those courageous businessmen who "go down in flames," and suffer the ignominy of an empty office, a kick upstairs, an early retirement. Somebody ought to establish an award for daring business pilots who flame out. This would surely encompass a large fraternity.

As with all successful businessmen, John cannot rest on his laurels. Right now, he is living somewhat uneasily with a new program that he dared recommend to the FTD board of directors. It calls for pioneering an application of electronic data-processing equipment in an untested area of retailing. For years, the FTD clearing house used the latest keypunchers, sorters, and computers of IBM and Honeywell to process orders exchanged between FTD members. It collected from one florist and paid the other at the same time, giving both parties weekly and monthly statements of all FTD transactions.

At John's suggestion, FTD is now offering its members a new computerized accounts-receivable billing system. Not only does the association process members' FTD orders, but it also processes *every* transaction in the shop. From sales slips which are optically scanned at the clearinghouse in Detroit, the association prepares all monthly invoices on EDP forms, sends them to the customer, provides the florist with a trial balance, and mails within five days of cut-off. All this for twenty-five cents a statement.

The programming costs for this new service were naturally very high. Furthermore, many FTD members resisted the innovation vigorously, especially because their bookkeepers worried that they would be put out of their jobs.

So far, the system has experienced innumerable problems from carbon failure, sales slip requirements to suit hundreds of individual shops, personnel training, equipment delivery delayed unbelievably beyond promised dates, delicate EDP equipment kicking up to the point that some manufacturers have thrown in the towel. Twice, the FTD board has taken steps to discontinue the program. It would have done so had not John Bodette personally dared to lay every success he ever gained in FTD on the line that the program will succeed.

It is still too early to tell whether it will. But as every businessman like John knows, there's no such thing as a plush-lined rut to crawl into if you want to be successful. Insecurity is one of the prices of daring to be different.

Bibliography

British Export Marketing Advisory Committee Appointed by the British National Export Council Committee for Exports to the U.S.A., Report of the (New York), May, 1967.

Brown, Helen Gurley, *Sex and the Single Girl* (New York: Bernard Geis Associates), 1962. *Sex and the Office* (New York: Bernard Geis Associates), 1963. *Outrageous Opinions* (New York: Bernard Geis Associates), 1966 (Los Angeles: *The Los Angeles Times*), 1963, 1964, 1965.

Brown, Stanley H., "Who's to Blame for Riklis?—Riklis?" *Fortune*, October, 1963.

Business Week, "Combining All Channels to Reach a Mass Public" (New York: McGraw-Hill, Inc.), September 18, 1965.

Carlesi, Paula, "Meshulam Riklis—Study in How to Make a Billion," *Women's Wear Daily*, February 27, 1967.

Carmody, Deirdre, "Free Bus Service Begins in Harlem," *The New York Times*, December 30, 1967.

Carroll, Jack, "The Feminine Evolution," *The Montreal Star*, July 15, 1967.

Chain Store Age, Variety Store/General Merchandise Edition, "MMG: Where It Is . . . and Where It's Headed" (Part 1 of 2 parts), October 1967. "MMG: The Next Step—Building Sales-Power" (Part 2 of 2 parts), November, 1967.

Chamberlain, John, "Lindsay Unwon By Negro Enterprise," *The New Haven Register*, January 18, 1968.

Cleveland Plain Dealer, The, "Harlem Self-Help Bus Defies Law," January 22, 1968. "Self-Help and Law Collide," January 23, 1968.

Combined Insurance Company of America, "1967 Annual Report."

Cox, Claire, "Become a Millionaire," *Dare*, May–June, 1965.

Crawford, Joan, with Jane Kesner Ardmore, *A Portrait of Joan* (New York: Doubleday & Co., Inc.), 1964.

Current Biography, James O'Neil (1947). Joan Crawford (New York: The H. W. Wilson Company), Vol. 27, No. 8, September 1966.

Daily News Record, "The Riklis Thesis," February 27, 1967.

Denton, Henry, "A City that Wouldn't Die," *The American Magazine*, August, 1937.

Dun's Review, "Meshulam Riklis: How to Build an Empire Without Cash," July, 1967.

Ehrlish, Blake, "Millionaire Tells Secret of His Success System," *Boston Traveler*, January 2, 1963.

Gelman, Morris J., "The Man Behind the Midas Touch," *Television Magazine*.

Graham, Virginia, with Jean Libman Block, *There Goes What's Her Name* (Englewood Cliffs: Prentice-Hall, Inc.), 1965.

Hill, Napoleon, and Stone, W. Clement, *Success Through a Positive Mental Attitude* (Englewood Cliffs: Prentice-Hall, Inc.), 1960.

Investor's Reader, "Communications, Metromedia's Media Mix," November 21, 1962. "Recreation, Metromedia Adds Class to Mass," September 22, 1965.

Kluge, John W., *Congressional Record, Senate,* October 28, 1963.

Leterman, Elmer G., *The Sale Begins When the Customer Says "No"* (New York: Greenberg, Publisher), 1953. *Personal Power Through Creative Selling* (New York: Harper & Row, Publishers), 1955. *The New Art of Selling* (New York: Harper & Row, Publishers), 1957. *How Showmanship Sells* (New York: Harper & Row, Publishers), 1965.

Maltz, Dr. Maxwell, *Psycho-Cybernetics* (Englewood Cliffs: Prentice-Hall, Inc.), 1960.

Matthew, Dr. Thomas W., Partial text of Opening Statement in "Debate on a Guaranteed Annual Income," at Overseas Press Club, February 16, 1967. "A Message from Dr. Matthew, February, 1966," *N.E.G.R.O. News,* September 2, 1967.

McCrory Corporation, "1966 Annual Report."

Metromedia, Inc., "1966 Annual Report."

Nash, C. C., "Personal Development of a Billion Dollar Producer," *Insurance,* September 9, 1967.

National Cyclopaedia, The, on Meshulam Riklis.

Phillips, Wendell, *Unknown Oman* (New York: David McKay Company, Inc.), 1966.

Pugh, Thomas, "Marines Land in Heart of Interfaith Hospital," *The Daily News,* December 24, 1966.

Robbins, Jack, "The Doctor Takes a Bus," *The New York Post,* January 4, 1968.

Rockey, Linda, "How to Get Along on $300 Million," *Chicago's American,* August 2, 1967.

Shepard, Richard F., "John W. Kluge: Man on the Go," *Television Age,* April 15, 1963.

Solow, Herbert, "The Drillings and Diggings of Dr. Phillips," *Fortune* magazine, February, 1957.

Standard & Poor's, *Standard A.S.E. Stock Reports,* October 3, 1967, October 26, 1967; *Standard Listed Stock Reports,* August 25, 1967, September 15, 1967, December 18, 1967; *Corporation Records, Regional Exchange Stock Reporter,* November 3, 1967.

Stapleton, R. W., "Soda Water in Margaret Street, The Story of Schweppervescence," *In Britain,* August, 1966.

Stone, W. Clement, *The Success System that Never Fails* (Englewood Cliffs: Prentice-Hall, Inc.), 1962. (With Norma Lee Browning), *The Other Side of the Mind* (Englewood Cliffs: Prentice-Hall, Inc.), 1964.

Variety, "Kluge Credo On Racial Equality in B'casting: 'Put Up or Shut Up'," September 11, 1963.

Welles, Chris, "Helen Gurley Brown Turns Editor," *Life* magazine, November 19, 1965.

Whitehead, Commander Edward, "How to Succeed By Really Trying," U.S. Naval Institute, June, 1965. "Who's Afraid of the Stars and Stripes?", *The Advertising Quarterly,* No. 5, Autumn, 1965. "The People Behind the Quality Image," *The Canadian Salesman,* March/April, 1966.

Index